RIFLEMAN

MILITARY ILLUSTRATED

RIFLEMAN

ELITE SOLDIERS OF THE WARS AGAINST NAPOLEON
WRITTEN BY PHILIPP ELLIOT-WRIGHT

SERIES EDITOR TIM NEWARK
COLOUR PLATES BY CHRISTA HOOK

Current titles
Marine
Stormtrooper
Rifleman
Highlander

Future titles
Ranger
SAS
Paratrooper
Commando

*To Richard Moore, the living embodiment of
the quintessential rifleman and a good friend*

First published in 2000 in Great Britain
by Publishing News Ltd

UK editorial office:
Military Illustrated, 39 Store Street,
London WC1E 7DB, Great Britain

Philipp Elliot-Wright has asserted his moral right
to be identified as the author of this work.

ISBN 1-903040-02-7

Designed by Glenn Howard

Printed and bound in Singapore under
the supervision of M.R.M. Graphics Ltd,
Winslow, Buckinghamshire

CONTENTS

BIRTH OF THE RIFLEMAN

Although the enduring image of the British soldier in the age of gunpowder is that of the redcoat armed with the much-loved Brown Bess musket, it is the handful of his green-coated comrades in the 'Rifles' for whom most legends and hero worship are reserved. Long before Bernard Cornwell began crafting the character of Richard Sharpe, the 95th Rifles were already familiar to those who had made the most cursory study of the Napoleonic Wars. Originating in an age of warfare where most soldiers were still trained to fight in close order formations, the individuality of the rifleman stood out.

From the start, in 1801, as the 'Experimental Rifle Corps', later the 95th Rifles, they were seen as an élite, specially raised, trained, equipped and armed to fight as skirmishers. Whereas their red-coated comrades were still subject to the lash and expected to obey orders without question, the Rifleman was encouraged to think for himself with officers trained to lead without recourse to corporal punishment. Furthermore, because the ranks of the Rifle corps were composed of men noted for their initiative and intelligence, the 95th has produced the single largest body of memoirs of any regiment in the Napoleonic Wars. Be it officers such as Kincaid, Leach, Simmons, Smith and Surtees, or enlisted men like Costello and the Harris', this cornucopia of personal accounts ensured that the *esprit de corps* of the 95th has been transferred down the ages.

But it was not just the special character of the 95th that ensured its place in popular imagination. Both its tactical role and the way it viewed the ordinary soldier made it very much the shape of things to come. Riflemen were trained to fight in what today is termed the tactics of 'Fire and Movement'. Whilst retaining a tactical cohesion, the component parts of any formation would use any cover to either move rapidly forward or back, dependent upon the flow of battle, whilst maintaining a highly accurate fire upon the enemy.

To ensure ordinary Riflemen were able to perform this tactical deployment, they were treated as thinking individuals who needed to be able to use their initiative in combination with disciplined team-work. Whilst ordinary line infantry always looked to their officer for any and all direction, the Rifleman was trained to operate in small groups, if necessary acting independently from his officer or senior NCO. Equally, the ordinary Rifleman was motivated to act not by fear of the lash but by the respect he received as a professional soldier and skilled marksman. Essentially, this is the ethos of today's infantryman.

The development of the 95th was the culmination of many decades of evolution. The concept of specially trained light infantry deployed to harass an enemy goes back to ancient times, whilst selected bodies of riflemen emerged in the Prussian Army fifty years before the fifth battalion of the 60th Royal Americans were formed in 1797 and the Experimental Rifle Corps first gathered at Horsham in 1801. However, if the British Army was relatively late in establishing such a formation, once the fifth battalion 60th and the 95th took the field, these sharpshooters provided a serious challenge to the feared French skirmishers, variously termed *tirailleurs* and *voltigeurs*, who nicknamed their new opponents 'the grasshoppers'. Furthermore, the 95th were to be integrated by one of history's greatest field commanders, the Duke of Wellington, into a tactical combination with their red-coated comrades that regularly defeated the best of the French Army.

So successful were the first rifle armed battalions of the 60th and 95th that within a few years two further battalions of each were raised. As the war progressed, additional rifle armed units were raised from bodies of German soldiers fighting with the British, of which the King's German Legion and Brunswick *Oels* are examples. Britain's Portuguese allies also armed a proportion of their light infantry regiments, the *Caçadores*, with rifles.

Finally, whilst all previously raised bodies of Riflemen had been disbanded at the conclusion of the wars they had valiantly fought in, the fifth Battalion 60th (Royal American) Regiment and the 95th Rifle Regiment established a permanent place in the British Army. In 1816, the 95th Rifles became the Rifle Brigade, whilst in 1824 the 60th became The Duke of York's Own Rifle Corps, later changed to the King's Royal Rifle Corps. Until the adoption of the Enfield rifled percussion musket in 1853, these two regiments remained the only rifle-armed infantry in the British Army. More importantly, they retained the unique character and training that had so distinguished them during the Napoleonic conflict so that even during the Crimean War the individual Rifleman's initiative enabled them to distinguish themselves in an otherwise difficult conflict.

If imitation is the sincerest form of flattery, across the Atlantic in the oft-claimed home of the Rifleman, the American Civil War saw the formation in 1861 of a green-coated regiment of 'elite' riflemen in the guise of Berdan's Sharpshooters. Armed with the newest breech-loading Sharps rifles, they were proof, just prior to all infantrymen being armed and trained as such, that the camps at Horsham, Blatchington and Shorncliffe had witnessed the birth of the modern soldier.

INVENTING THE RIFLE

From the moment the first projectile in Europe was propelled by a charge of black powder from a barrel some time in the 13th century, the search was on to improve the performance of this new technology. Experimentation produced better mixes of components to produce more powerful gunpowder of a consistent quality, new methods of mixing and casting metals produced stronger cannon barrels and ever lighter hand-guns. However, as all these weapons were smoothbore, continued improvements in the sciences of chemistry and metallurgy ensured musket and cannon balls were propelled ever further, but there was no corresponding improvement in accuracy. This did not necessarily inhibit the role of the cannon, but for the handgun improved accuracy would make a difference. While the early musket or arquebus of the fifteenth century could already propel a lead ball with sufficient energy to kill and maim up to 250 to 300 yards, it was a lucky musketeer who hit what he aimed at much above 40 to 50 yards.

This relatively poor performance was not significantly improved throughout the entire history of the smoothbore musket. Firstly, the lead balls did not perfectly fit the bore of the barrel, meaning they bounced up the barrel, leaving at whatever angle the last bounce imparted. Furthermore, the balls themselves were not perfectly cast nor the barrels truly smooth, the former being thus deflected in the direction of any imperfection. Other than improvements in the consistency and power of gunpowder, the basic physics of a smoothbore barrel discharging a lead ball meant that the redcoat at Waterloo firing his Brown Bess held a weapon whose ballistic performance was nearly identical to the musketeer at Bicocca and Pavia three hundred years before.

The apparent gap in the improvement of military ballistics from the sixteenth century onwards was not because science was unaware of the solution. Professional gun-makers knew early on that the setting of feathers at an angle on longbow arrows and crossbow bolts imparted a spin in flight that gave greater accuracy. While this led to experimentation with firing arrows from tubes, at some point around 1500 an unknown gunsmith in central Europe discovered that, if parallel spiral groves were cut along the length of the bore of a barrel, the spin they imparted to the projectile increased both accuracy and velocity. The spiral grooves caused the imperfectly cast lead ball to spin, thus imparting an artificial equilibrium that enabled the ball to travel in a far straighter line. Further, the spiral grooves held the ball more tightly

The highly intricate inlay on the stock of this German hunting rifle c.1600, exemplifies the élite status of the early rifles, restricted to hunting aristocrats.
Wallace Collection

Britain had its own version
of border troops in the form
of its Highland companies.
First raised in the early
18th century, by the time
of the War of the Austrian
Succession they constituted
the British Army's first
regiment of light troops.

Next page, by 1800, the
Prussian Army fielded an
entire regiment of *Jäger*.
Illustrated by Knotel as they
appeared in 1806, when
despite the general failure
of the Prussian Army to
defeat the French, they
made a distinct impression
on Napoleon's finest.

than in a smoothbore barrel, so that as gunpowder progressively combusted, a greater pressure built up behind the ball imparting a higher exit velocity. The result was the world's first known rifle, a matchlock, made for Emperor Maximillian I sometime between 1500-19.

There was a major problem, however, in handing this improved technology to the common soldier-- expense. All metal objects were hand-made by skilled craftsmen prior to the Industrial Revolution and while smoothbore musket barrels could be manufactured in quantity for an acceptable cost, the higher quality of metal and skill required to hand-cut grooves along the inner surface of the tube made rifles the preserve of the wealthy. By the early 17th century, the land-owning aristocracy and gentry of Europe were able to purchase fine quality rifled wheellock and flintlock hunting rifles capable of hitting game with accuracy at distances up to 200 yards. The cost of such weapons meant their appearance in war was a notable exception and then almost entirely in sieges for sniping.

The performance of the common smoothbore meant musketry was only effective if fired in mass volleys from troops standing shoulder to shoulder in linear formation, three to five ranks deep. Thus by the early 18th century, the infantry of all European armies utilised linear tactics that permitted the greatest amount of concentrated and continuous firepower, the individual soldier being drilled to load and fire mechanically as rapidly as possible. The bayonet was considered an instrument of shock that was expected to carry a massed infantry assault at the final moment of impact by demoralising the enemy and causing him to flee. Hence it was not obvious that a few hundred expensively armed sharpshooters would make any notable difference to the course of a major battle involving massed ranks of tens of thousands. Equally, the fact a muzzle-loaded rifle took a considerable time to reload ensured their rate of fire was very low in comparison to the smoothbore musket and the advance of any substantial body of formed infantry or cavalry could easily drive them off.

It was also understood from early on that any body of rifle-armed skirmishers would require specialist training and a degree of battlefield independence that would stand in sharp contrast to the main body of infantry. Prejudice and doubt as to whether the average farm labourer, who made up the bulk of 17th and 18th century armies, would be capable of developing the initiative and skill to operate in detached groups were added to questions as to whether the considerable expense of arming them with rifles would bring any

Whilst he despised irregular light infantry fielded by the Habsburgs, Frederick the Great recognised the potential of rifle armed marksmen and pioneered the establishment of highly capable Prussian *Jäger*. Initially raised from skilled gamekeepers and hunters, Britain was to model its own riflemen on these green-coated troops half a century later.

***Right**, with its short heavy barrel, the traditional German Büchse (hunting rifle), was the key to the Jäger's armoury. Their short length yet high level of accuracy made them ideal for combat in forest and undergrowth.*

identifiable benefit. To put it bluntly, the standard infantryman of the 1700s was cheap, effective and was constrained within the tight confines of the established military hierarchy. The concept of giving the common man an expensive rifle, capable of doing little more than pick off their social betters was anathema to the established military profession.

FRONTIER WILD MEN

Despite these problems associated with rifles and riflemen, the more general concept of light troops was becoming slowly recognised by the early 18th century as a useful support to serried ranks of line infantry. The concept of some form of lightly armed soldiers moving ahead of the main body of more heavily armed troops was hardly new. In almost any military establishment where there were distinct military roles, types of soldiers that might be described as skirmishers had featured.

In the ancient world, the lightly armed Thracian *Peltasts* and Spartan *Helots* acted to protect the early heavily armed warriors in the phalanx from enemy cavalry and skirmishers, as later the early Roman legions were screened by *Leves* and *Velites*. Whether *Peltasts*, *Helots*, *Leves* or *Velites*, these lightly armed spearmen who skirmished with an enemy prior to the engagement of heavy infantry would have found the tactics of light infantry two thousand years later quite familiar.

By the early 17th century, armies were deploying small bodies of troops termed 'piquets' at a short distance from the main body to screen an army from the opposition and to act as a trip-wire that could provide adequate warning and intelligence of an approaching enemy. However, once battle was joined, all returned to the ranks and combat was decided by formations relying on fire and shock tactics. The only exception to this was the 'war of outposts' or *petite guerre*. This recognised that small bodies of troops, be they mounted or on foot, could usefully engage in harassment of an enemy by raids on lines of communication and supply whilst living off the land. This though was seen as only a minor aspect of the greater whole and as having no significant impact on major battles and sieges.

The source for such troops came from the wilder frontiers of European nations and their empires such as the highlands of Britain, the forests and mountains of French Canada and the Balkan borders of the Habsburgs. Given the nature of the landscape and the availability of hardy locals able to move and fight in such wooded and mountainous terrain, units of 'irregulars' who fought in open order and served under a somewhat informal standard of discipline were a familiar aspect of military life by the mid-18th century. Such units of irregulars were viewed by the respective military establishments as strictly a product of their native environment and initially there was no concept that they might have a role in more formal theatres of war or a permanent place in the regular forces. It was from these units, however, that battlefield light infantry and riflemen emerged in the second half of the 18th century.

Louis XIV of France was one of the first to incorporate formally such troops into his army, formations of Hungarian light horsemen serving as early as 1692. By the 1700s, the Hungarian *Hussar* was already a familiar figure of fear for many civilian populations and an annoyance for armies in the field as various forces used them to stage raids and engage in general harassment. Hungarian *Hussars*, however, were light cavalry and it was not until the War of the Austrian Succession (1741-47) that an infantry version of such troops began to find a place. Since the 16th century, Serbo-Croat military colonists in 'military borders' had settled the Balkan frontier between the Habsburg and Ottoman empires. In return for land, almost the entire male population was liable for a feudal mode of military service against Turkish incursions.

Both life in general and military service in particular were arduous in the extreme and the

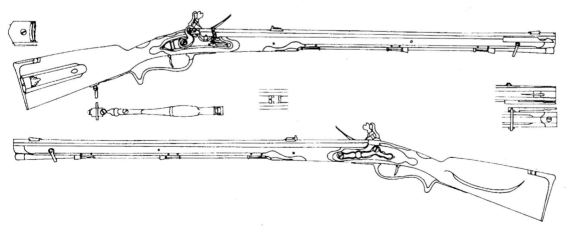

troops of the military border, termed *Grenzer* ('borderers') were inured to hardship and skilled in the irregular nature of frontier warfare. Even by the 17th century, the term Croat and Pandour had come to denote a brutal type of mercenary adept in raids and ambushes. The Austrians, wishing to utilise their tough border troops against Frederick the Great, brought regiments of *Grenzer* north. Raised on centuries of raids, massacres, persecution and assassination, these irregulars were familiar with a vicious style of warfare that commonly involved rape, plunder and murder.

Under such brutal leaders as Trenck, Nadasti and Loudon, these regiments brought a style of conflict to German civilians not seen since the worst excesses of the Thirty Years War. However, they quickly proved invaluable in the broader scope of *petite guerre* – reconnaissance, outpost work, screening the army and staging ambushes. Austrian generals soon found that such light infantry were also able to cover and protect large formations of ponderous line infantry during major engagements, whilst proving excellent sharpshooters with the very long muskets they carried on the fringes of battle.

The military impact of the *Grenzer* was soon recognised by other armies and by 1745 the French Army under Marshal de Saxe fielded various formations of light infantry. Consequently, at the Battle of Fontenoy in April 1745, Cumberland's British and Hanoverian soldiers found the numerous copses of trees and enclosures they had to negotiate to assault the main French lines were swarming with light troops. With no skirmishers of his own to drive them out, Cumberland's troops had to accept the heavy toll of casualties these French light troops exacted before they were forced back by the sheer weight of numbers of the Allied columns.

At this stage, it is ironic that the only light infantry Cumberland could call upon were the recently formed 43rd Highlanders, the Black Watch.

Independent companies of Highlanders loyal to the government had been raised as far back as 1710. Whilst the various Jacobite insurrections had caused them to be periodically disbanded, as early as 1725 four companies of Highlanders had become known as the Black Watch. The inhabitants of a rugged and harsh 'frontier' that compared to that of their *Grenzer* counterparts, they were uniquely equipped to operate as a fast moving police force to keep the Highlands of Scotland under some degree of control on behalf of the British Government. In 1739, eight independent Highland companies were combined to become the 43rd Foot (it was renumbered the 42nd in 1749 due to the reduction of General Oglethorpe's Regiment) and it joined Cumberland's Army in Flanders in 1743.

The Highlanders were expected to serve as a lightly equipped striking force, capable of undertaking rapid marches, rather than serving as battlefield skirmishers, but in battle, although equipped to act as light troops and having the necessary 'native' skills to do so, they were utilised as a standard regiment of infantry, formed up shoulder to shoulder. They were not even present on the field at Fontenoy, being detailed to guard the Army's baggage some miles to the rear. While Cumberland was to raise and utilise successfully various other regiments of light troops during the war for scouting purposes and the like, despite suffering at the hands of French light infantry, at the conclusion of the war in 1748 all were disbanded. To be fair, this practice was common to every European army. Essentially, the established military hierarchy still saw light troops as a purely wartime necessity.

Thus the Seven Years War commenced with bodies of irregular light troops being raised from scratch. However, both in the formal theatre of conflict in Germany and in the colonial theatres in North America and India, light troops soon proved crucial to the success of operations. This resulted in

Opposite, British and Hessian Riflemen during the American War of Independence. The summer of 1778 witnessed a number of clashes in the forests of New Jersey between American Riflemen versus British light infantry and Hessian *Jäger*. In this painting, having wound open its breech plug, the British officer reloads his Ferguson rifle, whilst Hessian *Jäger* engage the advancing men of Morgan's Rifle Corps with their short heavy muzzle-loaded rifles.

The British officer wears a severely cut-down version of the uniform, making it suitable for fighting in the dense North American undergrowth. All metallic lace has been removed and he is not wearing his distinctive gorget, epaulets or sash that would identify his rank to the enemy. The Hessian *Jäger* were strongly influenced by their Prussian brethren, their dark green coat with crimson facings, cowhide haversack and leather equipment being essentially identical.

Equally so was their rifle, whose short length was easy to handle and load in undergrowth, although its thick octagonal barrel made it a heavy weapon overall. The men of Morgan's Rifle Corps wore hunting shirts known as 'rifle frocks' and were armed with the long barrelled 'Kentucky' rifle. Whilst highly accurate, it proved less than sturdy for military field service. *Painting by Christa Hook.*

Although this Victorian print is highly stylised, it does convey the devastating tactics that shattered Braddock's command and triggered a radical re-think in respect of light troops amongst some British officers.

the foundation of permanent bodies of light troops and the growing recognition of them as a distinct and specialised body of soldiers. In the European theatre it was, as ever, the Austrians who were the first to field their *Grenzer* whilst the French soon raised various units of light troops. Frederick the Great, however, had an utter disdain for such troops, believing they were at worst an irritant who fled in the face of a resolute body of regular Prussian infantry. Thus, unlike either the French or British Armies, he had chosen not to raise them during the War of Austrian Succession, but with the coming of the Seven Years War this changed, as *Grenzer* again harassed Prussian supply lines and terrorised the civilian population. This time it was Frederick's subjects who were suffering. Further, at the battle of Kolin in June 1757, the despised *Grenzer* inflicted severe damage on Frederick's infantry to which he had no effective response. Consequently Frederick, finally recognising the need for light troops both on and off the battlefield, ordered the raising of his own *Frei-Corps* ('free corps'), mercenary bands of irregular light troops similar to those fielded by the Austrians, often deserters from Austrian units attracted by higher rates of pay. Thus even the most hardened opponent of light infantry came finally to appreciate their utility.

THE FIRST RIFLEMEN

Whilst light infantry had been a long time coming to the Prussian Army, Frederick the Great took the lead in the establishment of a regular unit of riflemen, the *Jäger*. Shortly after his accession, while firmly dismissive of the *Grenzer* type of light troops, Frederick promoted the concept that small bodies of disciplined troops armed with rifles under regular officers could play a valuable role both on and off the battlefield. The first step in this direction came in 1740 when a force of 60 *Guiden* were raised in order to protect reconnaissance parties and to act as guides for regular troops through

broken and enclosed terrain. Soon after, in November 1740, Joachim Scheneck was appointed Frederick's *Capitain des Guides*. He was given the job of obtaining 'good guides and [to] hold them ready, so that when the army advances or a detachment is sent out, the troops may be accompanied by reliable guides who know all the roads and passages'.

Rapidly Scheneck raised a tiny 50-man mounted *Feldjäger-Corps zu Pferde* that rose by 1744 to a strength of 6 officers and 112 rank and file, raised from skilled foresters and hunters. From the start, both the *Guiden* and mounted *Feldjäger* wore green uniforms and were armed with the characteristic German *Büchse* (hunting rifle). This was a largebore rifled carbine with a faceted barrel that had evolved in the context of the thickly wooded German countryside with the objective of having sufficient accuracy and stopping power to bring down a charging boar. These first two small units, having proved their utility as guides, scouts and couriers, evolved in July 1744 into a force of 200 rangers divided into two companies clothed in green, the *Feldjäger-Corps zu Fuss*. In February 1757 they were increased in strength to 300 men and by October 1760 they had been augmented to a full battalion of 800. In addition to the regular army *Jäger*, by the late 1750s, several of the newly raised *Frei-Corps* also included detachments of *Jäger*.

Given the existing use of the rifle, it comes as no surprise to discover that gamekeepers, hunters and woodsmen made up the majority of these first military riflemen. Specifically selected as good shots, attributes such as agility, intelligence and self-reliance were also demanded. This set the *Jäger* apart from all other infantry where strict obedience to orders and the rapidity of loading was emphasised. A significant proportion of their officers were untitled, reflecting that even in Frederick's almost entirely aristocratic officer force, there was a clear appreciation of the need for

Recreated Woodlands
Indian of the type who
ambushed Braddock's
men. These warriors
were some of the world's
finest light troops.

Recreated redcoats of
the type who set out with
General Braddock into
the depths of the American
forests in 1755, wholly
unprepared to face
French irregulars and
their Indian allies

specialist leadership skills when commanding *Jäger*. It ought to be added however that the *Jäger's* first commander, Major von Baader, was so corrupt and incompetent that Seydlitz ultimately broke his sword and ripped the symbols of rank from his shoulder whilst on parade.

As the Seven Years War progressed, Frederick's *Jäger* proved their worth, expanding their role beyond that of just scouting and conducting patrols. Given the quality of the rank and file, they were sometimes employed on confidential missions; in 1756, Frederick planned to utilise Polish-speaking *Jäger* to move in disguise through Russian lines so he could maintain contact between Saxony and Berlin. More crucially for the future, they fought in a number of successful defensive engagements in woods and villages, evolving a coherent body of skirmish tactics and deployments suitable to riflemen. In October 1758, at the battle of Hochkirch, they fought on open ground for the first time. However, whilst evolving the tactics that would become familiar to future generations of riflemen, they also demonstrated their limitations. At an action near Spandau on 10 October 1760, Cossacks caught the whole battalion in the open. Due to their rifles' slow rate of fire and lacking bayonets, the *Jäger* were cut to pieces, a pointer to the crucial weakness of all units of marksmen left exposed on the battlefield.

Whilst the tactical use of such troops was still in its infancy, the impact of the Prussian *Jäger* was such that both the Austrians and Russians copied them, raising their own companies of *Jäger* in 1758. It must be stressed though that there was a crucial distinction to be made between Frederick's *Jäger* and those of his opponents. The Prussian *Jäger* were a small, élite unit of professional marksmen, entirely armed with highly accurate rifles and skilled in scouting and skirmishing. In the Austrian *Jäger*, only the rear third rank and NCOs carried rifles, whilst in the Russian Army only a handful had them, the majority carrying ordinary smoothbore muskets. Further, neither Austrian or Russian *Jäger* were trained in the skills of scouting or skirmishing, and marksmanship was ignored. In fact the Austrians treated their *Jäger* as only a wartime expedient, disbanding them in 1763, albeit reforming them later. In contrast and despite the disaster at Spandau, the Prussian *Jäger* were here to stay, rising by 1784 to be a full regiment of 10 companies, all highly skilled in marksmanship and skirmishing.

BRITAIN'S OWN RIFLEMEN

The wake-up call for the British Army, regarding the need for a regular force of light infantry, came at the Battle of Monongahela River in June 1755. Major-General Edward Braddock set out with some 1,450 men to attack the most important of the French outposts on the Ohio, Fort Duquesne. Whilst the forty-five year old Braddock had proved a quite capable officer in Europe and his British regulars were well drilled, he was completely unfamiliar with forest warfare. There were skilled woodsmen in his army in the guise of colonial Rangers available (the most famous of these being the company, later a full battalion, raised in 1756 by Captain Robert Rogers), but the majority of local troops that Braddock took were recently mustered Virginia Militia under one Colonel George Washington.

Having successfully hacked their way through thick forest, Braddock and his men reached the more open country of Little Meadows. It was here, on the wooded slopes above the River Monongahela, that 80 French regulars with 46 Canadian militia and 647 Indians, under the command of Captain Lienard de Beaujeu, ambushed the British column. With only their formal training available, the redcoats had little option but to stand in close order linear formation delivering volleys against an enemy darting from tree to tree and bush to bush. The result was inevitable as more and more officers fell to aimed

By 1757, officers such as Thomas Gage and William Howe had established highly capable bodies of light troops whose training and equipment was carefully tailored to the needs of forest warfare.

BIRTH OF THE RIFLEMAN

fire and disorder spread. At least 977 British and colonial troops fell, including Braddock, against just 12 French and 27 Indian warriors. The shocked survivors were fortunate to escape this massacre as the Indians fell to looting and scalping.

Although the British Army had, as so often in its history, to learn the lesson the hard way, Monongahela was sufficient to bring about dramatic and fundamental changes that would ultimately win the colonial conflict. It was one of the officers at the sharp end of the disaster on the Monongahela that now played one of the crucial roles in the evolution of light infantry in the British Army. Lieutenant-Colonel Thomas Gage had been in command of the vanguard and witnessed how, despite the fact Braddock had taken every precaution available, there were simply not the troops with the appropriate training or equipment to meet the demands of such warfare. With the full support of his senior officers, he set about raising a specialist regiment of light infantry--the 80th Foot.

Meanwhile, back in Britain, as an immediate measure to address the obvious gap, the British Army's original light infantry, the 42nd Highlanders, were dispatched and a '2nd Highland Battalion', the 78th Foot (later known as Fraser's Highlanders), was raised specifically for service in North America. Equally, the Duke of Cumberland resorted to the familiar method of raising light infantry by turning to a number of foreign mercenaries to provide suitable soldiers from the existing backwoodsmen of the frontier. Three Swiss soldiers of fortune, then serving as officers in the Dutch Army, were commissioned on 25 December 1755 to raise a four-battalion regiment. Having recruited 40 German officers as well as British, this nucleus sailed for Pennsylvania to fill out the ranks with suitable colonials.

Titled Loudon's Royal Americans, the very real fear of French and Indian deprivations ensured the ranks were quickly filled with German and English settlers. Following the existing model of Austrian

Opposite, **Major Robert Rogers became a legendary figure during the French Indian Wars. His Rangers were in the tradition of the wartime irregulars familiar to European armies.**

and French irregulars raised in the previous war, these professional officers of fortune built on the existing woodland skills of their men to create a highly effective regiment of over 4,000 light infantry. However, as the Royal Americans included significant numbers of English, Scots and Irish officers, it was not categorised as a foreign corps but as regulars and was numbered as the 62nd Foot on the British Establishment.

Although the majority of the Royal Americans were armed with the smoothbore Brown Bess musket, albeit the lighter version with a shorter barrel, there are various references in contemporary documents to a significant proportion carrying rifles of one description or another. In fact, as early as 1754, the Board of Ordnance had issued to troops about to depart for America a 'dozen of Rifled Barrel Carbines' from existing stocks in the Tower. As the nature of the conflict became clear, the Board of Ordnance provided quantities of German *Jäger* rifles along with 'light' muskets. Equally, many of the locally raised troops already owned their own or soon procured them. In June 1758, Lieutenant-Colonel Bouquet of the Royal Americans certainly commented to General Forbes that 'A large part of the provincials are armed with grooved rifles...' However, in the same letter Bouquet made clear one of the crucial problems with the muzzle-loaded rifle. Whilst it was preferable for them to keep the powder, greased patches and shot separate, rather than use ready-made cartridges as per the smoothbore musket, it did make for a slow rate of fire, particularly in wooded terrain.

Whilst, in time, the Royal Americans would find a permanent place in the British Army, at this time all these formations were strictly in keeping with the established practice of raising light infantry only in time of war from suitable frontier settlers. Of more long-term importance were the serving British officers who now introduced light infantry into every regiment in North America. Defying his reputation

The highly capable military professional, Colonel Henry Bouquet, was one of three Swiss officers employed to raise what became the British Army's first regular regiment of light infantry not disbanded at the conclusion of the war, The Royal American Regiment.

as a hidebound reactionary, the Duke of Cumberland, in 1756, wrote to the British commander in North America, the Earl of Loudon that 'till Regular officers with men that they trust, learn to beat the woods, and act as Irregulars, you will never gain any certain Intelligence of the Enemy'. Receptive to such comments, various officers, including Loudon, Gage, Amherst and Wolfe, all contributed to the formation of units of light infantry and the promotion of its role.

Of equal note for the future, the records show that by 1759 the proportion of light troops of one type or another issued with rifles, officially provided by the Board of Ordnance, was significant. For example, General Sir Jeffrey Amherst ordered that year that the wide variety of rifles previously acquired on an *ad hoc* basis by his troops be returned and instead the single 'official' model be issued. These were described as rifled carbines of .68 calibre (the term carbine at this period did not necessarily mean a short barrelled musket, but was a distinct category of 'lighter' weapon usually of smaller calibre than the standard .75). These were issued in varying numbers to the Royal Highlanders, the Royal Americans, the Light Armed Foot and the light infantry companies of the Royals, the Inniskillings, Abercrombie's and Murray's regiments. However, come the conclusion of hostilities, with the possible exception of those held by the Royal Americans, all were returned to the Tower and many sold at auction as early as 1764.

RIFLEMEN DEVELOPED

The lessons learned by the British regarding light infantry in the 1750s were also accepted in the French Army, where the Duke Victor-François de Broglie raised a special corps of *chasseurs* trained to fight in extended order. In 1760, a company of *chasseurs* became a permanent body of specialist light troops in every French infantry regiment and in 1788 12 battalions of *chasseurs* were raised. However, it should be

noted that all French *chasseurs* were only armed with standard smoothbore muskets. The peculiar French prejudice against the rifle was to remain a theme in the evolution of their light troops well into the early 19th century and was one shared by Napoleon.

Although at the end of the Seven Years War it would appear the previous policy of disbanding all specially raised regiments was again instituted in the British Army with the reduction of the light infantry regiments, along with irregulars such as Rogers' Rangers, appearances would be misleading. The Royal Americans, now re-numbered the 60th, were retained on the Regular Establishment to guard the frontier in North America. Furthermore, incorporating both the lessons of America as well as established European practice, all battalions of infantry were ordered in 1771 to raise a company of light infantry composed of their most active and agile men, where initiative over dumb obedience was to be valued. Most importantly, the post-war generation of senior officers, whose active service had been in North America, had taken its lessons to heart.

The key figure here was Major-General William Howe who both produced the first universal British light infantry drill and ensured it was adopted by all regiments in North America. Previously there had only been a selection of privately published works: Major Robert Rogers had published his *Journals* in 1765, whose highly vivid accounts of reconnaissance patrols and raids provided a useful guide to the requirements of guerrilla warfare. Rogers' *Journal* even provided a chapter on the rules for training regular soldiers to 'the ranging-discipline' on light infantry tactics. William Smith's *Ohio Expedition*, relating Bouquet's campaign of 1763-64 against the Indians of the Ohio Valley, provided details of light infantry equipment, training and tactics. The most complete of the privately published works, though, was Roger Stevenson's *Instructions for Officers Detached* published in

Opposite, **when rebellion broke out in the Thirteen Colonies in 1775, the American woodsmen, generally armed with long hunting rifles made an immediate impact as they inflicted heavy losses on officers, NCOs and drummers of the British Army.**

1771. Stevenson, a regimental officer of considerable experience, wrote his Instructions with the belief that all officers should be familiar with the tactics of the *petite guerre*. Consequently, the duties of reconnaissance, raids, ambushes, skirmishing and the attacking and defending of posts, fortifying villages and buildings were all detailed. However, whilst all the preceding were valuable in themselves, there was no official guidance for any officer wishing to train his men as light infantry and various *ad hoc* systems proliferated. With the directive in 1771 to form light infantry companies in every battalion, this became an issue that Lord Howe now faced.

During August and September 1774, various light infantry companies were assembled in a special camp near Salisbury under his direction. Here Howe trained them in a system of skirmishing and rapid manoeuvres designed in light of his experiences in 1757-59 in North America. Howe subsequently strove to spread his system of light infantry drill throughout the Army to ensure a uniform system that would enable companies to be detached from their parent regiments and combined into composite light battalions. It was Howe's *Discipline* that trained battalions to march and fight in two ranks rather than three, and to do so in open order (a full arm's distance between each file). These 'loose files' enabled movements to be carried out either at the quick step or at a run. Marksmanship, 'irregular and bush fighting' were all stressed, soldiers at Salisbury being issued the extravagant amount of ninety blank and twenty live rounds each for practice to ensure realism as well as accuracy. All this was to enable them to manoeuvre and fire in accordance with the 1764 *Regulations* while dispersed in open or extended order.

When Howe was ordered to America at the end of 1774 as second in command to General Thomas Gage, he used his position to alter the tactical training of all British infantry stationed there, regardless of whether they were light troops, line or grenadiers. Although there was only a limited period of time prior to the outbreak of hostilities to undertake this process, it is clear most troops were familiar with it. After Bunker Hill, when Howe took over from Gage, it became compulsory. Howe's *Discipline* was well suited to the wooded and generally broken terrain of the colonies, and whilst hardly perfect, it permitted British troops to move quickly whilst retaining tactical cohesion and maximising firepower.

AMERICAN WAR OF INDEPENDENCE

Howe's training stood the British troops in good stead when the American War of Independence erupted in 1775, and excepting setbacks such as Bunker Hill, enabled the redcoats to win a string of victories against Washington's Continentals. It would be fair to say that the senior officers of the British Army were, by 1775, already fully conversant with both the need for light infantry and their role. However, there still remained a tendency for the light companies to be creamed off into combined light battalions, thus denuding the line regiments of their specialist skirmishers. This led some battalions to cover this deficiency by identifying the best marksmen in each company as 'flankers' and using them as unofficial skirmishers.

If the Seven Years War had finally convinced the British officer corps of the need for light infantry and tactics suitable for skirmishing, the proof being the American War of Independence, then it was the latter conflict that fully introduced the rifle as a necessary weapon. Whilst British officers had served alongside Prussian *Jäger* during the Seven Years War in Germany, there had been no moves to introduce such troops permanently into the British Army. This does not mean the potential benefits of the rifle were ignored as a certain Patrick Ferguson was experimenting with a breech-loading rifle at least a year before the outbreak of conflict in North America.

If there had been any doubt amongst British officers as to the military efficacy of the rifle, the opening shots of the American War of Independence blew them away. Unlike Britain, where the rifle was the preserve of the landed classes, it was a relatively common weapon in the thirteen colonies. The large number of Dutch, German and Swiss settlers who arrived during the 18th century and settled, particularly in Pennsylvania, included numerous skilled gunmakers practised in constructing rifles. They soon found a ready market, both amongst homesteaders who needed an accurate weapon to ensure their families would eat and frontiersmen who required the ability to hunt small animals for their rich pelts.

Although the colonists admired the German style of *Jäger* rifle, it was a heavy weapon that required a large lead ball and a significant charge of powder. Given the cost of lead and powder, and the desire for a lighter weapon to carry on long forays through the dense forests of North America, German gunmakers resorted to the simple expedient of stretching the barrel and reducing the calibre. This allowed for a thinner barrel that reduced the rifle's overall weight with the added bonus of using less lead and powder. These long-barrelled (ranging between 40 to 50 inches on average) colonial hunting weapons were quite capable of downing a target at upwards of 300 yards. Although such weapons have been given the colloquial label 'Kentucky' rifles, the first use of this name was not until after 1815 and throughout, most were made in Pennsylvania. These were civilian hunting weapons, however, and they lacked both the robust construction of a military weapon and any provision for fixing a bayonet. The former ensured only the most skilled riflemen were capable of maintaining the weapon in the field, whilst the latter left colonial riflemen at a critical disadvantage if their opponents closed with them. In the opening stages of the war neither of these critical issues were obvious, but the significant number of British casualties at Lexington, Concord and Bunker Hill were.

Reacting to the heavy losses inflicted by the rifle-armed Continentals in the opening stages of the conflict, the Board of Ordnance quickly sought out supplies of German *Jäger* rifles, some of which were issued to men of the light companies of the Guards. By January 1776, an order for 200 rifles was placed with a British agent in Hanover whilst a further 800 were ordered from Birmingham gunmakers to be manufactured to an official Ordnance pattern piece made by William Grice. Equally, significant efforts were made to acquire the high quality of powder required by rifles. Come the spring of 1776, after only 100 German and 100 Birmingham rifles had been delivered, a completely new type of 'British' rifle emerged that occasioned a change of plans by the Board of Ordnance and an immediate halt to any further production of muzzle-loading rifles.

FERGUSON'S RIFLE
Born in 1744, Patrick Ferguson, the second son of an Aberdeenshire laird, was a typical representative of the many Scottish officers that made up a crucial element in the British Army. From his earliest days he was destined for military service, being sent as an adolescent to study gunnery, fortifications and

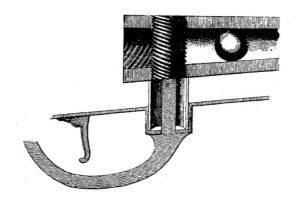

Originating with the breech-loading system devised by the French engineer and gunsmith Isaac de la Chaumette, Patrick Ferguson enhanced the design to produce the world's first workable military breech-loading rifle.

other military subjects in a private military academy in London. At fifteen, through the military influence of his mother's brother, Major-General James Murray, he gained a Cornet's commission in the Royal North British Dragoons. He subsequently saw action in Germany and Tobago, where tropical fever obliged him to return home. It was now that this thirty-year-old professional soldier demonstrated that he had a gifted technical mind as he used his enforced period of idleness to study a recently patented breech-loading rifle.

Throughout the 17th and 18th centuries, prompted by the wealthy sporting market, various gunmakers had been attempting to perfect an effective breech-loading rifle. Quite early on it was recognised that a plug that could be unscrewed from the breech was an obvious answer. The problem was that, to ensure an airtight seal, the screw had to be firmly seated, a time-consuming fabrication process given all parts had to be hand-tooled. Furthermore, whether the plug was inserted on top, at the side, or underneath the barrel, once unscrewed the plug had to be placed somewhere safe whilst the cartridge was loaded before being replaced, another time-consuming and tricky process.

It was a Parisian Huguenot gunmaker, Isaac de la Chaumette, who invented in 1704 a new system of breech-loading that offered an effective solution whereby the screwed plug passed from the top of the barrel through the breech and was attached to the trigger guard below. With a single 360-degree turn of the trigger guard, the plug was screwed down to open the breech but no further. The sportsman had to load his powder and ball into the open breech before turning the trigger guard back round to seal it firmly. Apart from priming the pan from a flask with fine powder, the rifle was ready to fire. In 1721 Chaumette became a refugee from a renewed spate of French persecution and emigrated to London, where he patented his design. Alongside fellow French gunmaker

Georges Bidet, he made a comfortable living selling his rifle to the landed classes.

Chaumette's design, however, had one significant flaw in that the male threads on the plug were easily fouled after only a few discharges. Whilst this was relatively unimportant in a sports gun where a gentleman's lackey was always available to keep it clean, alongside the rifle's high unit cost, it made it unsuitable as a military weapon. There is no record of the Board of Ordnance ever even testing it, Viscount Townsend, Master General of the Ordnance, commenting that it was 'liable to clog and when out of order is very difficult to be mended or replaced in the hurry of service'. It was to these issues that Ferguson turned his attention in 1774. In 1776, Ferguson was successful in patenting a modified Chaumette rifle with four innovations.

Ferguson added a projection of the barrel towards the guard so the plug could descend sufficiently low to enable the grooves to be fully cleaned without the need to remove fully the plug (this had previously entailed the awkward task of re-seating the plug). The face of the plug that formed the rear of the breech, once the rifle was loaded, was also smoothed off and hollowed out so that the combusted remains of powder did not lodge in the female screw. A similar smooth-faced hollow was created behind the screw plug to receive smoke and debris, which was forced back through the grooves and could be easily cleaned out when the plug was lowered. Finally, small channels were cut through the head of the plug so that when it was twisted down, they acted to loosen and receive dirt and other debris on the female screw.

Having completed his prototype and patented it, Ferguson utilised his mother's military contacts to afford him the opportunity to demonstrate his rifle before the King at Windsor where he discharged six aimed shots in one minute. Shortly afterwards he performed a second demonstration for the Board of Ordnance at Woolwich despite heavy rain and

John Simcoe was amongst the most influential of a new generation of capable British officers skilled in light infantry tactics produced by the American War of Independence. His leadership of the Queen's Rangers and subsequent writings helped highlight the need for specialist light troops.

high winds. For both the King and the Board of Ordnance, Ferguson proved himself a born salesman, hitting the centre of his target from various prone and standing positions. That Ferguson was now successful in persuading the usually conservative Board of Ordnance to agree to the manufacture of 100 of these expensive rifles (twice the unit cost of a standard smoothbore Brown Bess) can be put down to a mixture of factors. Royal patronage was crucial, as was the fact that Ferguson was a well-connected military officer and recognised firearms expert. Finally, and possibly most crucially, the outbreak of the American War of Independence ensured an identifiable military role, given the nature of the theatre and the already prevalent high reputation and fear of the American rifleman.

Having secured the manufacture of his rifle by early 1777, Ferguson now secured the raising of a special company to use it. It was recognised that special training and skilled marksmanship were crucial if the weapon's potential were to be realised. Consequently, and partially countering the myth of a blinkered military establishment, Captain Ferguson was detached from the 70th Foot and authorised by the Secretary for War, Viscount Barrington, to select 100 soldiers from the 6th and 14th Foot at Chatham Barracks to raise a 'Corps of Riflemen'. After intensive training, Ferguson's Riflemen arrived in New York on 24 May 1777, bringing with them a supply of green cloth for uniforms (unfortunately there is no other surviving record of their uniform). Ferguson's Riflemen subsequently participated in a number of skirmishes in New Jersey prior to the opening of Howe's Philadelphia Campaign.

Howe already had a body of Riflemen in the guise of units of Hessian and Anspach *Jäger* whom he had brigaded into a powerful advance guard of combined battalions of light infantry and grenadiers, both composite formations drawn from the élite companies of the infantry. However, when the Army landed on the banks of the Elk River on

The green-coated Queen's Rangers were amongst the finest light troops in the British Army. Although few if any carried rifles, in many respects they were the forerunners of the fifth battalion 60th and 95th twenty years later.

25 August, Howe divided the Army into two grand divisions for the march on Philadelphia. He attached Ferguson's Riflemen to that headed by the Hessian commander, Baron Wilhelm von Knyphausen, whilst the Hessian *Jäger* and the 2nd Battalion Light Infantry acted as the vanguard of the other under Lord Charles Cornwallis.

The campaign was to provide Ferguson's Riflemen with a brief but memorable record of active service. On 11 September at the Battle of Brandywine, Ferguson's 80 surviving riflemen fought alongside the 400 men of the renowned regiment of Loyalist light infantry, the Queen's Rangers under Major Wemys, as Knyphausen's

Daniel Morgan was easily the finest officer of rifles in the American War, and amongst Washington's most capable generals. Yet even his élite regiment of riflemen was forced to retire in haste in the face of a formed and determined body of troops.

vanguard. Ferguson and Wemys' men saw the most fighting that day of Knyphausen's command, successfully driving the 650 men of General William Maxwell's Continental Corps of Light Infantry back across Brandywine Creek. The combat was fierce, first a series of skirmishes from one defensive point to another, followed by an assault across Brandywine Creek at Chad's Ford in the face of both infantry and artillery. While victorious, the intensity of the fighting can be gauged from the fact the Ferguson's 80-strong corps suffered 40 casualties whilst the Queen's Rangers had 14 officers and 130 men killed and wounded. Unfortunately for Ferguson, he was seriously wounded when a rifle ball shattered his right elbow. It should be noted that the vanguard of the other grand division under Cornwallis was equally successful in defeating Washington's light troops.

Although Ferguson's able subordinate, the prominent New York Loyalist John de Lancey took command, Ferguson's incapacity, the heavy losses the unit had suffered and the fact that de Lancey was a Loyalist officer on the Provincial Establishment, proved the corps' undoing. Knyphausen recommended that it be disbanded and Howe, doubting the military effectiveness of a body of less than 50 men, agreed. The surviving soldiers were returned to the light companies of their original regiments and the rifles put into storage. Ferguson was furious but powerless to prevent this premature end to the British Army's first experiment with its own Rifle corps of regular soldiers. As for his 100 rifles, they have disappeared from the record. Those examples that now exist in various museums were individual pieces of high quality made specially for officers.

Before leaving the story of Ferguson's rifle, it is important to dismiss the oft-repeated myth that it was the great missed opportunity for British victory in America. Whilst there is no doubt his rifle was a remarkable weapon, it was not flawless and its faults were a direct product of its breech-loading mechanism. Firstly, to produce a high rate of fire the operation of the rifle required a significant level of skill and training. This linked to its second drawback in that it did not take a standard cartridge, requiring a ball of .68 calibre rather than .75 for the Brown Bess, and a higher quality powder, thus imposing a supply constraint, particularly in combat if the rate of fire was high. Finally, but most crucially, to accommodate the thicker breech with its screw plug, the wooden stock had to be further cut away at its very narrowest point. The result has been identified in the surviving examples of the rifle in that the weapon cracked easily across the stock between the lock and the trigger guard.

Thus, Ferguson's rifle failed the two crucial requirements of any infantry weapon: that it be easy to use and rugged enough to cope with the misuse and abuse of the ordinary soldier. Added to this is the simple fact they were expensive to manufacture: £4 each with bayonet compared to just under £2 for a standard Brown Bess with bayonet. It was these facts, and not the myth that British Army officers rejected the weapon out of 'fear' it would be adopted by the enemy or attitudes that it was not 'sporting' for weapons of war to have such accuracy, that ensured the demise of the Ferguson rifle. However, none of this should detract from the fact that Ferguson had briefly created the British Regular Army's first corps of Riflemen who could be seen as the forerunner of the 95th Rifles twenty-five years later.

RIFLE PROBLEMS

After the reduction of Ferguson's corps, there still remained a considerable number of units armed with more traditional muzzle-loading rifles. Since 1776, Hessian and Brunswick *Jäger* (modelled on the Prussian *Jäger*) had been part of the larger body of paid mercenary troops brought over to fill out British ranks--there were some Riflemen in the 60th Foot, albeit an undetermined number and

several of the Loyalist units had a proportion of Riflemen, but again specific numbers are unclear. It may be wondered, given the early concern over American riflemen in the aftermath of Lexington, Bunker Hill and other small actions, why more British and Loyalist troops were not armed with muzzle-loading rifles, which were now readily available? The answer is important as the proportion of rifle-armed soldiers was to remain small, even during the Napoleonic wars when British industry was quite capable of producing large numbers of relatively affordable rifled weapons.

The fact is that very rapidly it was realised that even the traditional muzzle-loading rifle had serious limitations that made it unsuitable for any form of stand-up fire fight and, by 1776, the war had taken on a more familiar style. In a series of battles between 1776-78--Long Island, Harlem Heights, White Plains, Brandywine Creek, Freeman's Farm, Bemis Heights and Monmouth-- whilst light infantry proved vital for scouting and skirmish purposes, combat was decided by two opposing bodies of infantry armed with smoothbore weapons and bayonets, drawn up in standard linear formation. It was much the same in the South between 1779-81, at battles such as Camden, Guilford Court House, Hobkirk's Hill and Eutaw Springs. On numerous occasions it was a classic bayonet charge by a red-coated line that cleared American marksmen from woods and bushes and drove their main bodies of troops from the field.

The problem for the muzzle-loading rifle was that it was much slower to reload than the smoothbore musket. Even a moderately trained infantryman could discharge a musket twice or even three times in a minute, being able to 'tap' load (provided the bore of the barrel was clean, the soldier need only bite open the cartridge, pour the powder down followed by the ball, and then strike the butt sharply on the ground to seat the ball) rather than use the ramrod. Even if the ball lodged part way down

the barrel, there was usually sufficient strength in the barrel to cope with the pressure wave while the soft lead ball was propelled out. None of this was possible with a rifle, particularly given the enormous pressure wave that would result if the ball was lodged only part way down and had to be driven through the grooves of the rifling.

Rather, having judged the distance to the target, the rifleman first had to measure out carefully a suitable charge of powder from his horn or flask before pouring it down the barrel. Next, to ensure the greatest accuracy, the lead ball had to be 'patched', that is to say, they were wrapped in linen, pigskin or calfskin patches that would be cut in a cross-shape so as to fit completely around the ball. These patches were lubricated with tallow or lard to ensure a tight fit and almost to eliminate windage (the escape of gas around the ball as it was propelled up the bore). Further, the patches assisted in reducing the amount of fouling from the part-combusted powder, thus keeping the bore clean. However, given the tight fit, the patched ball had to be driven firmly by the ramrod down the rifling to seat in the breech. Finally, the rifle's flash-pan was primed with fine powder before a careful aim could be taken. It therefore took at least one, if not two, minutes to reload even for the most skilled. Although not an issue while skirmishing in open order or sniping from cover, this was not the decisive weapon to secure victory on any open battlefield.

Despite their reputation, even the vast majority of Washington's Continentals were armed with smoothbore muskets. There were élite American Rifle corps, such as Colonel Daniel Morgan's, described by General John Burgoyne after his defeat at Saratoga, as 'the finest regiment in the world'. However, there are two cautionary tales to be told that reveal the limitation of riflemen in general and civilian-made muzzle-loaded rifles in particular. One of various post-war commentators reflecting on events in America was a Colonel George Hanger, who had served throughout the conflict with the Hessian *Jäger* and Loyalist irregulars. Writing to the British Foreign Secretary, Lord Castlereagh, in 1808, he commented generally that: 'Riflemen, as riflemen only, are a very feeble foe, and not to be trusted alone any distance from camp; and at the outposts they must ever be supported by regulars, or they will be constantly beaten in, and compelled to retire on the main army.'

To illustrate this, Hanger referred to a notable clash in Pennsylvania between a force of British light infantry armed with smoothbores under Colonel Abercrombie and Morgan's Riflemen. As Morgan's men appeared from some broken and wooded ground, Abercrombie 'ordered his troops to charge them with the bayonet; not one man of them, out of four, had time to fire and those that did had not time given them to load again; they did not stand three minutes; the light infantry not only dispersed them instantly, but drove them for miles over the country: they never attacked... our light infantry again, without a regular force to support them.' It is interesting to note that even Washington issued a strict standing order that Riflemen were only to be deployed in circumstances where they could safely retreat having discharged their first shot.

Whilst part of the reason for Morgan's Riflemen being at a disadvantage was their lack of support from a substantial formed body of troops, the very nature of the American colonial rifle left much to be desired as a military weapon, particularly its lack of a bayonet. A particular clash in 1778 illustrates why the short-barrelled German *Jäger* model (that could take a sword bayonet) was to be preferred when it came to establishing a British Rifle corps 20 years later. On 3 January 1778, General Hugh Mercer led a raid on a British outpost outside Philadelphia defended by Lieutenant-Colonel Charles Mawhood's brigade. Most of Mercer's command were riflemen, the combined veterans of various Virginia, Maryland and Delaware regiments, supported by a brigade of militia under Cadwalader.

As Mercer advanced, Mawhood was in the process of marching one of his regiments, the 17th Foot, to join Cornwallis at Trenton. Although only screened by a handful of light dragoons, these still managed to spot Mercer's men and, pre-warned, Mawhood quickly marched the 17th back down the road towards Princeton and the rest of his brigade. Before being cut off by the rapidly advancing Americans, Mawhood raced to occupy a small hill alongside the Princeton road. Mercer's men were closer and won the race. A classic encounter action now ensued between two veteran forces both numbering around 400 men. Mercer's brigade deployed into a ragged line behind a rail fence and began to fire. Mawhood did not hesitate: the 17th also deployed into line and delivered a volley. Although this mostly went harmlessly over the Americans' heads, the 17th now charged forward with fixed bayonets.

As the 17th swarmed up the hill and over the rail fence, the American Riflemen had no chance to fire more than once and were then in deep trouble as it was not possible to fix a bayonet to their long-barrelled civilian hunting rifle. In moments, it was all over as Mercer's men were fearfully cut up. Those that did not flee were bayoneted, the latter fate proving fatal for Mercer himself. Having successfully captured the hill, the 17th was now assaulted by Cadwalader's brigade, but a single volley was sufficient to send Cadwalader's militia fleeing to the rear. Ultimately the 17th was overwhelmed and forced to flee as Washington personally rallied both Mercer and Cadwalader's men and brought up fresh troops. The vulnerability of unsupported riflemen armed only with long-barrelled rifles was again clearly demonstrated, even when they had occupied the high ground.

While the rifle had yet to establish a permanent place, the British Army had, by 1783, adapted itself to the demands of light infantry warfare. The combined experience of conquering Canada and then losing the thirteen colonies meant the majority of serving British officers of all grades had learnt drill and tactics suited to the North American theatre. Three-rank deep formations had given way to two, with dangerously open intervals between files. Concentrated volley fire had been sacrificed for the sake of speedy movements. However, the dawning of the French Revolutionary Wars saw a return to more formal European warfare. In his influential 1788 *Principles of Military Movements,* General Sir David Dundas, who was to write the 1792 Regulations that would take the British Army through the Napoleonic Wars, wrote critically of the over-emphasis on light infantry to the detriment of heavy infantry: 'The battalions… have been taught to undervalue themselves, and almost to forget that in their steadiness and efforts the decision of events depends, and that light infantry, *Jägers*, marksmen, riflemen, etc etc vanish before the solid movements of the line.'

Dundas wrote that the American experience 'has much tended to introduce the present loose and irregular system of our infantry'. This led to the tactical weakness of British infantry that was deployed in a 'very thin and extended order to make more show' and that sought to move with 'an affected extreme of quickness on all occasions'. Consequently, when he drafted the 1792 *Rules and Regulations for the Formations, Field-Exercise, and Movements, of His Majesty's Forces,* Dundas, whilst fully aware of the need for good light infantry, was guided by a wish to restore the role of heavy infantry – of the book's 458 pages, just nine were dedicated to light infantry. Hence, while it is another myth that Dundas rejected the crucial role played by light infantry, the British Army entered the Continental conflict in 1793 with the emphasis firmly on disciplined bodies of infantry drawn up in linear formation and trained to deliver concentrated volleys of musket fire. The reality, however, was that light infantry and riflemen in particular were to feature more strongly in the British Army as the war against Napoleon progressed.

ARMING THE RIFLEMAN

FRENCH DEVELOPMENTS

As the armies of Europe marched to war in 1792, all accepted the role of light infantry and most battalions of infantry had companies trained and equipped for that purpose. It is thus easy to overstate the impact of the French 'hordes' of light troops and skirmishers who were supposed to have swarmed over their conservative and inflexible opponents drawn up in old-fashioned close order linear formations.

Impressed by the continuous string of victories being won by French troops in the early 1790s, various contemporary writers often exaggerated or misinterpreted the actual situation. For example, there was the old and respected professional soldier, General John Money, who, having concluded his service in the French Army in 1793, retired to England. He subsequently wrote a series of open letters in the mid-1790s to the then Secretary-at-War, William Windham, on his interpretations of French victory. This later became a small booklet, *On a Partial Reorganization of the British Army*, published in January 1799. Money, who had only seen the 'new' French Army in action in 1792 before his retirement, commented on how they had advanced '*en masse*' which 'was nothing more than very large bodies of Irregulars, which covered the country, in the front of their Armies, like an inundation'. Money spoke of how it was 'to their Irregulars...are the French indebted for most of their victories'.

Money gave away his own mid-18th century antecedents in how he viewed these new French 'Irregulars'. Money, like many other veteran officers, the bulk of whose experience had been in the Seven Years War and American War of Independence, interpreted the large screens of infantry skirmishing forward of the main French lines as irregulars in the spirit of the Austrian *Grenzer* and American frontiersmen. The reality was that between 1793-94, whilst France was being invaded, there was little time to train the vast influx of new troops beyond the basics of small arms drill. French generals were forced to resort to various expedients. Unable to risk semi-trained troops in open country, where solid bodies of well-drilled troops were vital, French commanders chose rough and broken ground where they could deploy their troops in the well-established second-best version of linear formation, that of an open skirmish order.

Far from demonstrating some new-found 'revolutionary' tactic in warfare, the 'clouds' of loose French skirmishers were a sign of weakness: they were difficult to control (often giving way to panic) and militarily it was an indecisive mode of fighting. While they could harass formed bodies of troops, pouring forth an impressive volume of fire whilst ammunition lasted, they could not break them: only a similarly well-drilled body of formed infantry could hope to do that. Furthermore, like all light troops, but especially the loose and ill-trained generalised 'clouds' of French skirmishers in 1793-94, they dare not advance beyond broken and enclosed terrain for fear of being ridden down by enemy cavalry or simply chased off by any formed body of infantry. Even a champion of dispersed skirmishing such as General Philibert Duhesme was careful to distinguish between untrained formless mobs, *grandes bandes*, and properly trained light infantry. Essentially, the much-trumpeted waves of French skirmishers of 1793-94 were seen by their commanders as a necessary evil, an inferior and regressive system of tactics, to be replaced by well-drilled formations screened by properly trained light infantry once time permitted.

In fact, since the mid-18th century, the Royal French Army had developed its own doctrines and regular corps of light infantry, culminating in 1788 with the formation of twelve battalions of specialist *chasseurs*, alongside the *chasseur* company that was organic to every infantry regiment. For decades, leading French military theorists, such as Duke Victor-François de Broglie,

Baron François de Mesnil-Durand and Count Jacques Guilbert stressed the role of light infantry, firmly integrating it with the tactical deployment of line and column. Reflecting many professional soldiers' prejudice against traditional irregular light infantry, all, particularly Guilbert in his highly influential 1772 *Essai Genéral de Tactique*, argued for properly trained light infantry that could be deployed to support fully the main battlefield formations. Indeed, there were far fewer debates over the role of light infantry after the Seven Years War than over the contrasting merits of deep column formation, *l'ordre profond*, and those favouring the linear *l'ordre mince*.

In 1775, to resolve this debate, the Duke de Broglie carried out experiments to establish which was superior. The result was the adoption of Guilbert's preferred option--a synthesis of column and line, *l'ordre mixte*, which equally stressed the integrated role of highly-trained light infantry as skirmishers. Guilbert's ideas were contained in the *Réglements* of 1791 that remained the standard French Army manual until 1830. Consequently the army of volunteers and later conscripts who swept across Europe from the mid-1790s were trained by cadres of the old Royal Army who were already well versed in light infantry tactics, supporting battalions drilled to change rapidly from column into line and vice versa. The *chasseurs, tiralleurs* and *voltigeurs* did not develop their excellence through some mythical natural genius set free by the Revolution but rather through hard training from professional soldiers utilising the drill and tactical doctrines of the *Ancien Régime*. If there was a 'natural genius' set free by the Revolution, it was that of a new generation of French generals who had risen through merit rather than birth, utilising their rich inheritance from the old Royal Army.

Prussian, Austrian and British armies had also absorbed the tactical lessons of the mid-18th century and developed their own doctrines and bodies of trained light infantry. It is true that only

Prussia and a handful of smaller German states such as Hanover yet possessed a specialist corps of rifle-armed *Jäger*, both the Russian and Austrian armies viewing their *Jäger* battalions as generalised light infantry, trained to screen deployments rather than act as trained sharpshooters. In both the Austrian and Russian armies, only around 10% of their *Jäger* were even armed with rifles, the remainder carrying smoothbore muskets of a slightly lighter construction than the standard infantry version.

Whilst Frederick the Great had organised for training and *esprit de corps* purposes a single regiment of *Jäger*, on campaign they were broken up into company-sized detachments to operate, like their Austrian and Russian counterparts, with much larger bodies of smoothbore-armed light infantry. Given the very slow rate of fire due to the difficulties of reloading, and the fact they were meant to be marksmen who fired aimed shots, they required the support of troops armed with smoothbore muskets capable of a much higher rate of fire. The actual proportion of Riflemen to smoothbore-armed light infantry and the tactical doctrines governing their deployment varied little between the Prussian, Austrian and Russian armies by the early 1790s.

It was the able Prussian officer, Hans von Yorck who, in his 1800 field instructions for the *Jäger*, outlined the quintessential mode of operation for riflemen on the battlefield: 'it is an irrevocable basic rule that the *Jäger* never hurries his fire, but always shoots with effect. It is an equally irrevocable rule that two *Jäger* always defend one another, that is, always act in groups of two-front and rear man. These two *Jäger* must at all times consider themselves as one body; one defends the other, so that when one man has fired and therefore is defenceless, the other has loaded and is capable of defensive action.' Essentially, Prussia, Austria and other German states were ahead of France in the integration of trained light infantry with

1. Colonel Francis Baron de Rottenberg, shown here in later years in the 'red' uniform of the 60th Royal Americans, was already recognised as a leading exponent on the use of riflemen when he was ordered to transform Hompesch's Light Infantry into the fifth battalion 60th. *Royal Green Jackets Museum*
2. The young Robert Craufurd is shown here wearing the uniform of Hompesch's Light Infantry which essentially became the uniform of the fifth battalion 60th.
3. This magnificent looking officer of the fifth battalion 60th reflects how the original uniform of Hompesch's Light Infantry was adapted (around 1798) with the addition of much silver lace, buttons and fashionable 'light infantry' embellishments, particularly the Tarleton helmet.
4. Colonel the Honourable William Stewart could rightly claim to be the true father of the 95th Rifles.

sharpshooters, and it was these states, not France, that Britain was about to copy.

BRITAIN'S LIGHT TROOPS

As has been seen, the British Army was far from blind to the need for specialist light infantry. The problem was that they were limited to only a company per battalion and there was no mention of riflemen whatsoever. Thus, when facing the French Army in the early 1790s, British generals had well-trained bodies of light infantry, but they were limited in number. Hence they were faced with the odious practice of having to detach them from their parent regiments to form combined light battalions, thus denuding the line troops of any organic bodies of light infantry. Furthermore, there was no specialist body of rifle-armed troops enjoyed by their German counterparts. All this was brought home for Britain in the Duke of York's ill-fated campaign in Flanders, 1793-95.

When British troops landed in Flanders, they entered a landscape fully enclosed by fences and hedges, a terrain ideally suited to the deployment of light troops. The Duke, despite much later criticism, attempted to compensate by resorting to the well-established tradition of raising numerous bodies of light troops from the local German and Dutch populations. Whilst varying in size and effectiveness, units such as the York Chasseurs, Waldstein's Chasseurs, Lowenstein's Fusiliers, Hompesch's Light Infantry and Bentinck's Corps, all included in their ranks soldiers armed with rifles. In particular, the York Chasseurs (also known as the York Rangers) were entirely armed as Riflemen and had been raised by one Captain Ramsey who had gained considerable experience during the American War of Independence leading such troops.

Officered mainly by French émigrés and with a predominantly German rank and file, its four companies of Riflemen particularly impressed the Duke of York (in whose honour they were named)

throughout the campaign, both in outpost work and in acting with the rearguard. All these troops, alongside the example set by the Prussian and Austrian *Jäger*, essentially proved their worth to many British officers. Crucially, many of these foreign Riflemen then returned with the British forces when they evacuated in 1795, being based for a while on the Isle of Wight. Many were then posted to the Caribbean, where their skills were required in the thick jungles and mountains of the islands. However, poor acclimatisation and hard service ensured most were killed by disease.

In the aftermath of Flanders, the Duke of York, having been appointed Commander-in-Chief, set about rectifying the situation in respect of light troops and set in train not only a significant increase in the number of specialist light infantry in the British Army but also the formation of rifle-armed corps. In March 1797, he dispatched a circular letter to all generals commanding districts, drawing their attention to the priority of training

This rifleman reflects the general look of the fifth battalion 60th shortly after it was armed with the Baker rifle as he is equipped with its distinctive sword bayonet.

1. Taken from Cooper's 1806 work, the next few plates reflect how riflemen were drilled in the crucial art of skirmishing. Here a company forms into loose files and then extended order.

2. Deploying into and from extended order was crucial to many manoeuvres.

3. Here a company deploys into skirmish line before a battalion drawn up in line.

4. 'Formation of the Chain'.

1

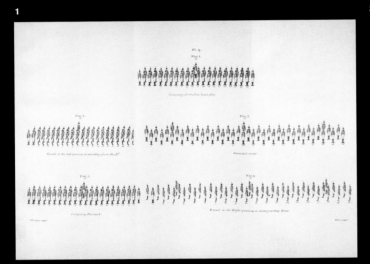

3

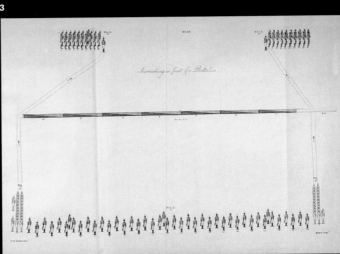

2

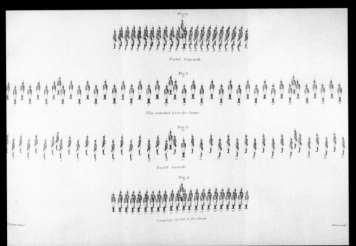

4

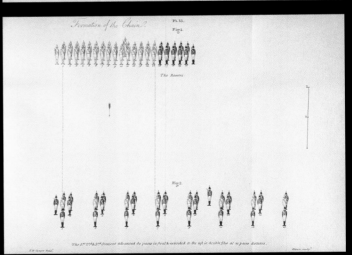

5. 'Firing Advancing'. Deployed in open order, each rifleman of the standard two-man file alternately moved forward, passing to his colleague's right.

6. 'Firing Retreating'. Essentially the same procedure, but in reverse.

7. The advanced guard in front of a Battalion.

8. 'Light Infantry masking the manoeuvre of a Battalion'.

5

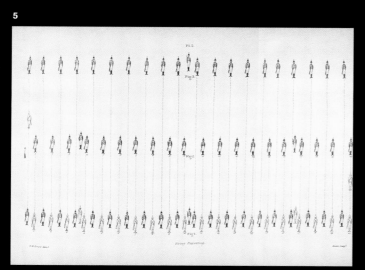

7

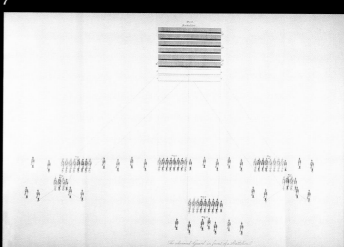

6

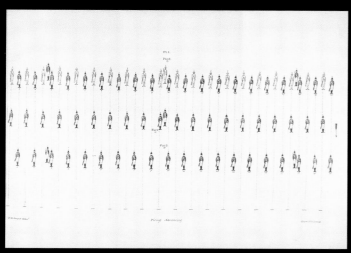

8

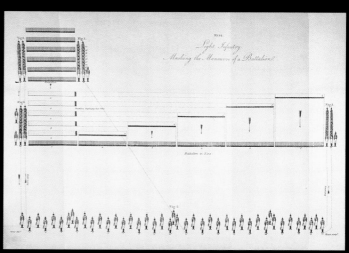

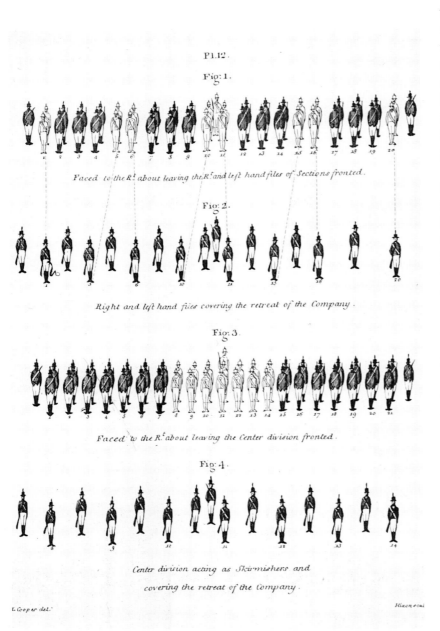

P1.12.

Fig: 1.

Faced to the R.t about leaving the R.t and left hand files of Sections fronted.

Fig: 2.

Right and left hand files covering the retreat of the Company.

Fig: 3.

Faced to the R.t about leaving the Center division fronted.

Fig: 4.

Center division acting as Skirmishers and covering the retreat of the Company.

L. Cooper del.   Hixon scul

Each company had to perfect complex drill manoeuvres: here the centre division acts as skirmishers to provide cover for the rest of the company.

light infantry companies, enclosing a copy of Dundas's light infantry exercise. In December he sent out a second circular on this subject requiring that all light infantry companies be 'diligently trained and perfected...in those movements and manoeuvres which are more particularly adapted to them...' as well as to receive practice in marksmanship. The Duke particularly highlighted the need for uniformity across the Army 'so that in case circumstances should at any time render it necessary to assemble and form them into distinct Battalions', it would be possible. Obviously this concept of forming special battalions of light infantry was not new, having been the normal practice for half a century.

During the summer of 1798 none other than General William Howe, who had done so much to train light infantry just prior to the American War of Independence, ran another camp in Essex for a similar purpose, albeit mostly for the militia. The logic of this need for companies of light infantry that were organic to all battalions of infantry, as well as entire battalions of specialist light infantry, resulted in the transformation of a number of regiments in Sir John Moore's camp at Shorncliffe.

FIFTH BATTALION, 60th ROYAL AMERICANS

It was finally decided in December 1797 to raise a fifth battalion for the 60th Royal Americans from the foreign, predominantly German, rifle corps still serving with British forces as a *Jäger* battalion. Here it must be stressed that, of course, Riflemen differed from the generality of light infantry in that they had a specialist role as sharpshooters. Whilst light infantry were expected to manoeuvre both dispersed as skirmishers and be able to fight in close order alongside regular line infantry, the Rifleman's function was to pick off enemy officers and NCOs and generally harass the enemy. They were to do this from protective cover or out of effective range of smoothbore muskets. The Duke of York had witnessed for himself the effect of the various corps of German *Jäger* who had fought with his army in Flanders. Since then the Duke had believed that, to bring the British Army up to the most modern standard of its Continental, and particularly Prussian and German counterparts, it needed its own corps of sharpshooters.

Initially, this fifth *'Jäger'* battalion was solely intended for service in North America where it was felt such troops would be of most utility. Consequently, on 30 December 1797, 17 officers and 300 rank and file of the *chasseur* companies of Hompesch's Light Infantry under their existing Lieutenant-Colonel, Baron Francis de Rottenberg, were so constituted. Hompesch's Light Infantry, which had various designations depending upon the source – Hompesch's Fusiliers and Chasseurs both being used – had been raised back in March 1796 by Ferdinand Hempesch in Germany. Clothed in green, the contract by which they were raised specified that the entire regiment was to be armed with carbines 'like the Prussian sharpshooters' and 10 men in each company were to carry rifled carbines.

Quartered on the Isle of Wight (at this time Roman Catholic émigré troops were not permitted to land on mainland Britain due to the still extant Test Acts), in October 1796, Colonel Nesbitt, the officer in charge of foreign units, gave them an excellent inspection report. By 1797, the regiment mustered 460 rifle-armed *chasseurs* and 690 fusiliers equipped with smoothbore muskets. Whilst the fusiliers were shipped off to the Caribbean, the *chasseur* companies remained on the Isle of Wight where they were subsequently re-mustered into four companies as the fifth battalion the 60th Royal Americans.

Rottenberg himself was not only to play a vital role in establishing the Rifleman in the British Army but also crucially contributed to the generality of training light infantry. Although born in Danzig, he joined the French Army in 1782 as a *sous-lieutenant* in the German *77eme Régiment*

These two files of recreated Riflemen show how, whilst the two kneeling reload, their comrades stand ready with loaded weapons.

(Le Marck). After the outbreak of the Revolution in 1789, foreign officers, particularly German, were viewed with suspicion and Rottenberg joined the wave of other émigrés departing France. Like many émigrés, he served in a variety of forces including those of Naples, then commanded a regiment of infantry in the wars between Poland and Russia, until he joined Hompesch's regiment in 1796. A talented officer, he rose quickly to be its Lieutenant-Colonel.

TRAINING AN ELITE

Once confirmed in his new role as commander of Britain's first fully rifle-armed battalion, albeit still 'foreign', Rottenberg immediately set about turning his men into a highly efficient force. An excellent organiser and disciplinarian, the simple but effective tactical system he drew up, *Regulations for the Exercise of Riflemen and Light Infantry, and Instructions for their Conduct in the Field*, soon gained a wider audience, despite being written in German. It was promptly translated into English by the Army's Adjutant-General, Sir William Fawcett, in 1798 and the Duke of York designated it the Army's official light infantry manual.

Rottenberg was guided by the earlier work of a German officer, Lieutenant-Colonel Johann von Ewald. Having commanded the second company of *chasseurs* of the Waldeck regiment in America, Ewald published in the early 1780s a detailed study of light infantry. This was promptly adopted as the main text for the training and tactics of the Hessian *Jäger* upon whom the later British rifle units would, in essence, be modelled. When Ewald moved to the Dutch Army, he produced an extended version of his work, *Abhandlung von dem Dienst der leichten Truppen*, for their light troops, where Rottenberg apparently became familiar with it.

Rottenberg, like Ewald and most other professional officers, had a well-founded contempt for the typical irregular forces that had been such a feature of light troops in the middle and latter 18th century. In training his Riflemen, he started with the assumption that only well-disciplined and trained troops could usefully serve on the field of battle. However, he was also convinced that, for any light infantry regiment, but especially Riflemen, to perform their functions fully, a strong *esprit de corps* was essential, particularly a powerful bond between the rank and file and their officers. The very essence of a Rifleman's role required they act in small, isolated groups, where both the highest level of training but also initiative was essential and where they had to have absolute mutual confidence in each other's abilities and support. Thus Rottenberg eschewed corporal punishment and never flogged a single Rifleman of his battalion; rather, according to the regimental historian Rigaud, he 'governed them in a patriarchal manner, more as a father would his children'. As most combat deployments involved the Riflemen operating in pairs, wherever possible Rottenberg allowed the soldiers to choose who they paired off with.

For officers, Rigaud relates that Rottenberg stressed they were to talk regularly with their men, 'hearing their opinion and sentiments on different subjects' and would thus 'learn the capacities and characters of their men that they may employ them to the best advantage'. Rottenberg equally built an intense regimental pride by promoting an intense awareness of both individual and general professionalism combined with a general regime of meritocracy. It was Rottenberg who first introduced the practice of permitting the best marksmen to wear special proficiency badges. This also paid off in terms of the Riflemen's physical condition and thus readiness for action. Rottenberg stressed the need for regular exercise and a high degree of personal hygiene, both being served by the spirit he engendered in his men.

Of course, none of this would have meant anything if the Riflemen were not indeed professional soldiers, highly trained and skilled

Opposite, the 95th Rifleman and his equipment. The uniform and equipment worn by the 95th Rifles in the Peninsula and at Waterloo was largely fixed by 1806 when the second pattern stovepipe shako was issued, made of blocked felt with a linen liner. Like the rest of the Army, Riflemen wore a black leather stock around their neck, held in place by a brass clasp. Whilst only the sleeves of the skirted jacket were lined, the insides of the fronts were faced with green cloth. The pointed cuffs were 2½ inches in breadth, whilst the 1802 regulations stipulated a 3-inch high collar. However, a circular letter from Horse Guards dated 5 August 1808 ordered that '…the collars of the Regimental Jackets should be made higher in the neck so as to entirely cover the clasp of the stock'. There were 12 buttons in each of the three rows down the front, set at equal distances apart. The rows were 7½ inches apart at the top, and reduced gradually to 2½ at the bottom.

Regarding equipment, the black leather cartridge box belt was 2½ inches in breadth from which the powder horn was suspended by a green cord. By 1806, the cartridge box or 'pouch' was capable of holding fifty rounds. The sword belt was made of the same black leather as the cartridge box belt and was also 2½ inches in breadth. It was fastened with a crude brass snake clasp. The ball bag that was hung from it could contain up to thirty-lead balls. The sword bayonet was the second pattern model of 1801 with a 23-inch long blade and brass handle. Although it gave the Rifleman a reach comparable to a full-length musket, its length ensured that when worn in its scabbard it often became caught between the Rifleman's legs when running, whilst when fitted the rifle became very unbalanced. However, it was excellent for cutting firewood, acting as a hook to hang lanterns from or for toasting food over a fire!

Other items of equipment included a wooden water bottle, a canvas haversack and wooden framed canvas backpack, all identical in construction and dimensions to those worn by the standard line infantryman. Finally, the Baker rifle introduced in 1806 was its 'third' pattern. It included a pistol grip trigger guard, a patch box with a plain rounded front and a flat steel lock plate and ring neck cock.
Painting by Christa Hook.

in their job, and in this Rottenberg excelled. Following his own Regulations, the Rifleman of the 60th was first 'taught how to hold himself, to march, face, wheel etc. as in regular infantry'. Then he was trained in marksmanship, practising against five to six-foot high targets of human dimensions. To ensure confidence was built, he began at a range of just 50 yards, gradually increasing by degree to between two and three hundred. Having become a proficient marksman whilst standing, he was then taught how to fire and load kneeling, sitting cross-legged 'as a tailor', and lying down on both his back and front. Finally, firing at moving targets mounted on sledges completed his skills as marksman.

Next the Rifleman was drilled in the various manoeuvres necessary to his role as sharpshooter and skirmisher. All movements were executed in 'quick time' of 120 paces per minute, each pace being measured at 30 inches. Formed up in a two-deep line, they learnt to extend their frontage to left or right whilst anchored by a file at the opposite end. Equally, the line could be extended out from the centre file whilst it stood firm. In whatever direction the line was being extended, its length was determined by the space left between each file. Depending upon the prevailing situation and frontage to be covered, there were three distances specified, 'loose files' that had a six-inch interval, 'open order' that had two-foot intervals and 'extended order' that had six-foot intervals.

Obviously, such an extended open order formation left the Rifleman vulnerable to attack. Consequently echoing Yorck, Rottenberg stipulated that at any given moment one of the two Riflemen in each file had to be loaded ready to give fire: 'Never more than half a body of Riflemen must be sent forward to skirmish, the other half remain formed and ready to support'. It was this requirement for a substantial formed body of troops to fall back on that dictated the deployment of any extended skirmish line.

The concluding element to the Rifleman's combat training was in the crucial evolutions that enabled him to combine firing with movement. Firstly, when facing an enemy on the battlefield, half the unit would form up in close order as a reserve, whilst the other half deployed in an extended two-deep line some 50 paces to the fore. The whole would then advance in quick time until the foremost skirmishers were within an appropriate range of the enemy (depending upon the broader tactical situation) when they would halt. The leading rifleman in each file would then, once ordered, take aim at his discretion and fire. Whilst he reloaded, the rifleman behind him would run past him on his right six paces forward. Once the Rifleman who was now the rear rank had completed loading, he would call out 'ready', allowing the Rifleman in front to fire. This process was continued until a halt was called and the line would then retire by the simple expedient of reversing the process.

When it was necessary to establish first contact with an enemy, a mode of deployment termed the 'chain' was used. Here the objective was 'to scour a tract of the country by means of numerous and detached bodies, clearing the woods and enclosures of the enemy's posts and, in a word, to establish a complete chain of your troops, by occupying, as far as circumstances will permit, every advantageous spot'. For this, three-quarters of the unit would be deployed in extended order, although now two files would operate together as 'divisions' with ten paces between each group of four Riflemen. The remaining quarter of the Riflemen remained formed as a reserve fifty paces back.

As Riflemen were likely to form part of the vanguard of an army, deployment to gather intelligence and acting to warn against ambush was another part of the training. Rottenberg taught that a vanguard ought firstly to comprise a 25-strong half-platoon deployed upwards of five hundred paces in front of the main force, three

Colonel Coote Manningham's lectures were a basic part of the Rifles' early teaching.

hundred paces if weather or light was poor. Two hundred paces beyond was another half-platoon, with an NCO and six men scouting another one hundred paces forward of this. Another half-platoon was deployed three hundred paces to either side covering the flanks with an NCO and his six men scouting one hundred paces forward and to each outer flank. Hence 120 Riflemen could both scout ahead on a frontage of around one thousand yards and to a depth of 800 paces beyond the front of the main body.

To be a fully proficient Rifleman, his skills were capped off with how to conduct patrols and the provision of sentries and piquets. The latter duties were crucial and involved the observation of the enemy and providing early warning of their approach whilst purchasing time by harassing them with rifle fire and, if possible harassing counter-attacks. This was achieved by a chain of paired sentries being deployed in front of the main body of the piquet, sufficiently far for them to be able to listen without being distracted by the noise emanating from their own side, yet sufficiently close to alert them easily if necessary.

To ensure the outlying sentries remained alert, an officer-led patrol continually did the rounds whilst the main body of the piquet rested with their arms stacked. If an enemy force did indeed approach, the outlying sentries signalled by firing their rifles. One of the paired sentries then ran back to the main body of the piquet to convey as much intelligence as circumstances permitted whilst the other stood his ground with the remainder of the sentries to buy time for the main body of the piquet to stand to. Having been alerted, they would stand-to-arms in their pairs, each pair being some six paces from the next pair, each firing and loading alternately whilst the remaining sentries retired and fell in. The piquet then maintained its fire until it could no longer hold its ground when it would either fall back by pairs to a position where a further stand could be made,

or until they were ordered to fall back behind the main body of troops.

Given that the Riflemen were carrying out tasks that inevitably placed them in dispersed deployments and moving with rapidity over various types of terrain, command and control was a serious issue. Consequently, the fifth battalion 60th, as would become the norm for the 95th Rifles, had a larger allocation of officers and NCOs at company level than a standard line regiment. Given the distances involved, and to ensure orders were received over the noise of battle, all officers carried whistles to signal their instructions for use when they felt their verbal order would not be heard by all their men. At regimental level, given that drums would have been impossible to carry at the rapid pace moved at in action, bugles were used. This meant that the ordinary Rifleman had to familiarise himself with both the various commands conveyed by whistle and separately by bugle. The whistle's calls were basic and limited to small unit deployments of less than a single company. Those from the bugle ran to 57 calls, to include orders to extend, halt, close ranks, charge, incline to the left or right, open fire, cease fire, retreat, disperse, and to form line, column or even square. There were also calls for passing intelligence when an enemy had been sighted and a description: infantry, cavalry or both.

RIFLE GREEN

The fifth battalion 60th were envisaged as a *Jäger* battalion in the German tradition and this was reflected in their uniform and equipment. Hence, as Hompesch's corps already wore a short, single-breasted deep green jacket with red collar and cuffs, green shoulder straps and wings piped red, along with blue breeches and black leather belts, this was retained and became the basis for the fifth battalion's distinctive uniform.

As for the ordinary Rifleman's weapon, many of

The magnificent officer's uniform of the 95th Rifles closely resembled that of their compatriots in the fifth battalion 60th. Distinguished by black velvet facings, the fashion-able Tarleton helmets, silver lace and fittings and three rows of silver ball-buttons down the front ensured officers of the Rifles were instantly recognisable.

Hompesch's German soldiers appear to have brought with them their short, thick-barrelled rifles, common to Continental *Jäger*. For those who required new weapons, however, the only British made rifles were those following the established pattern of 'light' muskets, these being essentially similar to the 39-inch barrelled India Pattern musket with rifling. These rifled muskets were rightly judged as unsuitable, hence the Board of Ordnance ordered in August 1798 5,000 Prussian *Jäger* rifles through Hamburg, using the agency of Paul and Haviland Le Mesurier. While upon delivery a significant proportion of these were found to be faulty (partially triggering the search for a suitable British-made version which resulted in the Baker rifle), there were sufficient sound weapons to satisfy the needs of Rottenberg's men.

Before the four companies of the fifth or '*Jäger*' battalion of the 60th could be dispatched to North America, rebellion erupted in Ireland. Rottenberg's Riflemen were judged to be an ideal corps for service against the Irish rebels, given the irregular, almost guerrilla-style of warfare involved. It should be noted that another corps by the name of Hompesch, namely a corps of Mounted Riflemen also known as Hompesch's *Chasseurs à Cheval* and Light Dragoons also served in Ireland at this time but were a totally separate body. In Ireland the four companies of the fifth battalion 60th '*Jägers*' formed part of a 'Light Brigade' under the command of Brigadier-General John Moore, an officer who was later to play a crucial role in the continuing evolution of British light troops.

After Ireland, the fifth battalion 60th was dispatched to the Caribbean where, in June 1799, having suffered losses at the capture of Surinam, it absorbed a further 33 officers and 600 rank and file from Lowenstein's *Chasseurs*, one of the surviving German corps raised back in 1795. The fifth battalion 60th, now stationed on Martinique, also absorbed further detachments from its original corps, Hompesch's Light Infantry, (the remainder of the regiment being absorbed by the red-coated second battalion of the 60th). Having now achieved its full establishment of ten companies, the fifth battalion 60th saw service in North America over the next few years, being stationed in Nova Scotia until ordered back to Britain in 1806.

So useful had the fifth battalion proved, that in 1799 a rifle company was attached to each of the red-coated battalions of the 60th: the first, second, third, fourth. At the same time, a further two battalions of Germans were raised to serve as Riflemen and dressed in green, becoming the sixth and seventh battalions of the 60th, (there is some

question as to whether the whole of the sixth battalion were immediately raised as Riflemen). These had a slightly varied uniform from the fifth battalion in that the sixth had deep green facings on the collar, cuffs and shoulder straps piped in red. Also, the sixth are shown in contemporary plates as commencing service with tan leather belts, only changing to black at a later date. As all served in the Caribbean, white mosquito trousers were worn. However, regardless of uniform details, by late 1799 the British Army, albeit in its 'foreign' regiment, the 60th, already had in excess of three battalions of Riflemen and the Duke of York needed little additional evidence that a specialist 'British' rifle corps was now long overdue.

EXPERIMENTAL RIFLE CORPS

In December 1799, the Duke of York announced that a camp for training elements of the regular army was required, including 'a Corps of Riflemen by detachments to be returned' to their battalions 'when properly instructed and the exercising of five Regiments together as a Light Corps'. However, the Duke was obliged to put this concept on ice when Dundas and Pitt required that a substantial force be dispatched to the Mediterranean on what proved to be a series of abortive attempts to attack Cadiz and support the Austrians in Italy. This was followed by the Peace of Amiens in 1802 that made the need for such efforts appear less crucial. It was only in 1803 as the war with France resumed and Napoleon began assembling his *Armée de Angleterre* at the Camp de Boulogne that York could justify assembling three battalions of light infantry at the camp at Shorncliffe under Sir John Moore.

Returning to January 1800, the Duke of York was determined to pursue his intention of establishing a specialist corps of British Riflemen, similar to the rifle-armed elements of the 60th, particularly as the latter were serving in the Caribbean and North America, where they were expected to remain. Having expressed this basic intention, the Duke already had a candidate to raise it, a Colonel Nightingall. At this point Lord Charles Cornwallis intervened, arguing strongly that just ten percent of any new corps should be armed with rifles. In promoting this option, Cornwallis was not arguing against the concept of specialist riflemen--his experience in America had convinced him of the power of marksmen. As has been previously noted, there was general agreement that *Jäger* were to operate only as part of the broader role of light infantry. Thus the debate here was between the Austrian model of having a mix of rifles and

Below left, for the rank and file, their uniform and equipment was again modelled on that of the fifth battalion 60th, distinguished by black facings. Note in particular the flask of powder suspended from the cartridge belt.

Below right, the same Rifleman viewed from the back shows how the hair was still expected to be worn clubbed into a queue. The short tails on the jacket can be clearly seen as can the unwieldy sword bayonet.

smoothbore weapons in each battalion of light infantry, or the Prussian model, where there was a single specialist corps of Riflemen who would support light infantry battalions.

Despite the success of Rottenberg's Riflemen in the 60th, essentially modelled on the Prussian and Hessian *Jäger*, the Duke was convinced by Cornwallis' arguments, particularly as it was based on considerable combat experience. Cornwallis quoted his experience in America where, due to the slow rate of fire from Riflemen, many corps that were initially only armed with rifles moved to a mix of smoothbores and rifles. This choice had even been made by the commander of the Hessian

Jäger, Lieutenant-Colonel Ludwig von Wurmb, who found his Riflemen were unable to match the volume of fire from his American smoothbore-armed opponents in many hard-fought skirmishes. The greater accuracy of each muzzle-loaded rifle shot failed to compensate for the three to four rounds each smoothbore could get off over the same period of time. Thus the Duke dropped the idea of forming a specialist regiment and instead opted for the concept of training just a small body of men from every battalion to act as sharpshooters.

Consequently, on 17 January 1800, fourteen regiments (2nd Battalion 1st Foot, the 21st, 23rd, 25th, 27th, 29th, 49th, 55th, 69th, 71st, 72nd, 79th, 85th and 92nd) were each ordered to detach 30 privates, two corporals, two sergeants, one ensign, one lieutenant and one captain respectively. '...that it is His Royal Highness the Commander-in-Chief's intention to form a corps of detachments from the different regiments of the line for the purpose of its being instructed in the use of the rifle and the system of exercise adopted by soldiers so armed'. Once trained, it was made clear they would return to their parent regiments to provide sharpshooters, whilst another fourteen regiments were to send detachments for training, the process to continue until every regiment had such a body of specialists.

Although the Duke's instructions directed that the regiments only detach 'such men as appear most capable of receiving the above instructions and most competent to the performance of the duty of Riflemen', the quality of those chosen was mixed. While some did select men of high quality, other colonels, despite knowing these men were ultimately to return, took the opportunity to unload some of their worst. By early February, eight of the detachments had duly assembled at the designated camp at Horsham, although the Duke had to prod the other six into sending theirs. Almost immediately the Duke had to notify five of the colonels that all 34 of the soldiers they had

Drawn from life soon after the formation of the Rifles, this picture undoubtedly inspired the two previous interpretations.

sent were 'unfit for Service' and required them to immediately dispatch 'good and serviceable men'. Various individuals from the other nine contingents also had to be returned for similar reasons. However, by late March 33 officers and 510 suitable rank and file had been assembled and work could commence, the first parade of the 'Experimental Corps' being held on 1 April.

The two officers selected to undertake the command and training of the 'Experimental Training Corps' were Colonel Coote Manningham and Lieutenant-Colonel the Honourable William Stewart. Whilst both played a key role in promoting the establishment of a rifle regiment in the British Army, it was the latter who was to ensure its success as a practical reality. Born in 1766, Coote Manningham was a veteran light infantry officer who had first entered the Army as an Ensign in the 39th Foot in 1782. A Captain in 1785, then Major of the 45th Foot in 1791, he was subsequently appointed to command one of the composite battalions of light infantry under General Sir George Grey in the Caribbean. It was Grey who had ordered this force assembled on Barbados in order to restore 'the perfection of Light Infantry attained during the American War', obliging every officer of the respective light companies to participate fully in a course of instruction. During his service in the Caribbean, Manningham had both observed and worked with various German émigrés units armed with rifles and had come to value their utility and skills. As early as 1800 he was giving lectures on the nature and use of rifle-armed troops in the field.

One of the young officers to participate in the light infantry training on Barbados had been the talented Scots officer, William Stewart. Like Manningham, Stewart had ample opportunity to hone his appreciation of light infantry and Riflemen whilst campaigning in the dense, lush, tropical undergrowth that covered most of the Caribbean islands' mountainous terrain. After returning from

the Caribbean in 1798, he was given leave to serve as an observer attached to the Austrian and Russian armies in Italy. Here he witnessed first hand the performance of both the skilled French skirmishers, but also the useful service performed by the Austrian *Jäger*. On his return, he proposed the formation of an 800-strong regiment of marksmen raised from Irish and Scots regiments volunteers. In certain respects, this reflected the traditional view of Highlanders as intrinsically more suited by temperament and upbringing to light infantry. Given these two officers' track record, they made a logical choice as commanders.

Having assembled the men and weeded out

Reflecting German influence, Sergeants were given far greater responsibility and were expected to display initiative.

those deemed to be unsuitable, in May the Experimental Corps was marched to the camp of exercise at Swinley, near Windsor Forest. Here they commenced an intense programme of training predicated on Rottenberg's *Regulations* and the recent work of another émigré, the Frenchman, General François Jarry. He had served under Frederick the Great as an ADC, been Governor of the Berlin *Kriegsakademie* and finally served under General Dumouriez back in France before emigrating. Recognised as a talented staff officer, in 1798 he became commandant of the recently established Military College at High Wycombe. In 1801 he wrote *Instructions Concerning the Duties of Light Infantry in the Field* that dealt with tactical guidelines for light infantry officers. Jarry's work so impressed the Duke of York he directed that it be a supplement to Rottenburg's *Regulations*.

Meanwhile, both Manningham and Stewart were writing to the Duke of York as early as 9 and 11 May respectively expressing their belief that the experimental training corps, such as it was, ought to be constituted as an established regiment. Whilst the Duke reiterated the intention to return the soldiers to their parent units, he strongly indicated that while 'the present is rather a corps of Experiment and Instruction and I trust its utility...' if all went well 'will ensure a similar one being formed on a permanent footing'. Despite Cornwallis's concerns, it seems obvious that the Duke ultimately intended to form a permanent corps of Riflemen.

Within two months of this exchange of correspondence, fate intervened in the form of a typical hare-brained scheme of Pitt and Dundas. In July the Duke was ordered to supply 13,000 troops for a combined action against the Spanish naval base at Ferrol. As Manningham's Riflemen were available, six of the regimental detachments were dispatched as a single unit under Stewart's command. On 25 August Stewart's men covered the expedition's landing on the north-west coast

of Spain, although the assault on Ferrol was aborted once it was found to be impregnable and the British promptly re-embarked. Whilst the whole adventure was an utter failure, it did ensure a proportion of Stewart's men served together as a coherent unit and 25 August, the day the regiment first came under fire, became the regiment's birthday.

Including those serving at Ferrol, the original personnel of the Experimental Corps were undergoing a major change. Of the original 482 soldiers assembled in March, 357 returned as originally intended to their parent regiments, the balance of some 70 men transferring permanently to what was already being termed the 'Rifle Corps'. To take their place on a more permanent footing, on 2 March, Horse Guards had issued a request that the 33 Fencible regiments based in Ireland each contribute 12 'active men as volunteers to the Rifle Corps...their services to be unlimited as to time and place'. A new camp had been established at Blatchington in Sussex in late August by the eight detachments not sent to Ferrol, and here they were joined by the volunteers from the Fencibles in Ireland, ultimately amounting to 396 men. At the same time, whilst the detached rank and file were beginning to return to their parent regiments, many of their officers chose to remain. In late October 1800, 26 officers were officially gazetted as belonging to 'A Corps of Riflemen', many of whom would later gain distinction in the Peninsula.

As the original Experimental Corps took on more of a permanent character, Manningham, now busy as an aide to the King, left Stewart, despite having been wounded at Ferrol, to undertake the corps training. Meanwhile the Duke seems to have made his mind up to constitute what was now, in practice, a regiment. With the green light to consider the Rifle Corps permanent, Stewart set about cementing its *esprit de corps* and establishing

The Green Book, a compilation of Stewart's Regulations and Manningham's lectures, became the basis of all training in the Rifles well into the 19th century.

the highest levels of training and discipline, taking his lead from Rottenberg. To ensure uniformity, Stewart set down the corps system of discipline, its chain of command and interior economy in a series of standing orders that were subsequently published under the title *Regulations for the Rifle Corps* formed at Blatchington Barracks under the command of Colonel Manningham, 15 August 1800. In this, Stewart sought to establish the spirit and identity that was to be the distinguishing mark of the British Rifleman.

SPIRIT OF THE RIFLEMAN

Like Rottenberg, Stewart started with the premise that for a corps of sharpshooters to operate as a professional body of marksmen, mutual respect and rationally thinking individuals were required. Thus, while Riflemen were to accept orders with 'deference and respect...whether he be an Officer or a Non-commissioned Officer, shall give his orders in the language of moderation and of regard to the feelings of the individual under his command; abuse, bad language or blows being positively forbid in the Regiment'. Corporal punishment was eschewed in favour of adornments to demonstrate prowess and merit.

Target practice was an everyday occurrence and competitions were regularly held to encourage marksmanship, with the best shots receiving a proficiency badge of white embroidered crossed rifles within a wreath on a dark green background. Stewart established some of the British Army's first regimental decorations, awarded for Good Conduct, Long Service and Special Merit. The last of these, a silver medal, was awarded for both bravery on the field but also 'voluntary acts of generosity towards either an enemy or those who are in an enemy's country'. Stewart recognised that, as much of the Rifleman's duty on campaign would entail outpost work and other isolated detachments, being on good terms with the local population was essential.

To encourage further responsibility, initiative and a desire to excel, 'In every half-platoon one soldier of merit will be selected, and upon him the charge of a squad devolves in the absence of both the Non-commissioned Officers of it. As from among these four Chosen Men (as they are to be called) all Corporals are to be appointed; the best men are alone to be selected for this distinction'. A white armband sewn to the upper right hand sleeve of their jacket denoted these Chosen Men.

Stewart made clear he expected that each company would form a military family under its captain, bound by ties of honour, comradeship and mutual confidence; he termed this the 'Company System'. 'In a Regiment of Rifle Men, each Company must be formed upon the principle of being separate from, and totally independent of another'. Consequently, to assist in building *esprit de corps* and a bond between the junior subalterns, NCOs and Riflemen, Stewart required that lieutenants, once appointed to a particular company, not be exchanged with another. 'This attention to retaining the same men and officers together is on account of Riflemen being liable to act very independently of each other and in numerous small detachments in the field when they will feel the comfort and utility of having their own Officer, Non-commissioned Officer and Comrades with them. The service will be benefited by the tie of friendship, which will more naturally subsist between them.'

Continuing this theme of establishing the closest possible bonds between the men, and taking his lead from the well-established German 'Comrade' system, Stewart had each company separated into two parts, with each of these being in turn subdivided into two with the officers, NCOs and Chosen Men proportioned equally between them. Next, keeping in mind that the ranks formed up two deep, 'guided' by the captain, each corporal, private and bugler selected a 'comrade' from the other rank. From then on they could only change

There is little doubt as to the inspiration for Ezekiel Baker, as this drawing of the Prussian *Neue Korps-Jägerbüchse* makes clear.

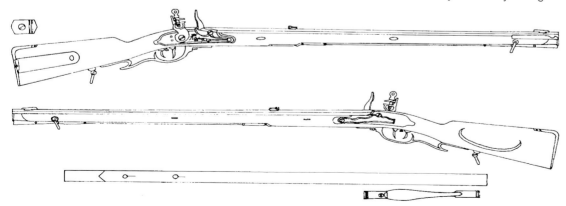

this arrangement with the express agreement of the captain, otherwise these comrades shared the same berth in quarters and formed the same file whenever the regiment was formed up. Given that Chosen Men were identified as potential corporals, Stewart encouraged they should team up as comrades. Once these pairings had been settled, the captain then established the messes.

This was a key issue for 'All messing is regarded by the Colonel as bearing a very important place in the good order and economy of a Regiment. Comfort and unanimity at meals, whether it be among officers or soldiers, is the source of friendship and good understanding'. For the rank and file, Stewart suggested 10-man squads were ideal, but never more than 17, each squad being headed by a corporal, seconded by an acting corporal or Chosen Man. Within each squad, a given mess would be of four men who would share a single camp-kettle for cooking their rations.

For the officers, Stewart insisted they all belong to a single mess, being both economical and, if any officer withdrew from it, it was a clear indication he no longer wished to serve with his brother officers and should leave the regiment forthwith. Finally, Stewart also insisted that all the sergeants mess together 'and on no occasion whatever with the Rank and File and Buglers'. For both the officers' and sergeants' messes Stewart held that it was the commanding officer's duty to make them 'comfortable and upon the most just terms of economy'.

Stewart recognised that to engender both self-respect and the ability to perform independently, education was vital. Given the generally poor to non-existent level of education of most common soldiers, he established a regimental library and a school of reading, writing, arithmetic and geometry 'for the instruction of those who wish to fit themselves for the situation of Non-commissioned Officers'. Both for instruction purposes and to foster further *esprit de corps*, Stewart had the

rank and file sit alongside their officers in lectures on light infantry drill and tactics.

Another crucial element of Stewart's work focused on the off-duty Rifleman when he sought to foster 'Exercise of Activity'. Hence the Regulations recommended that organised games were 'particularly characteristic of a light corps'. Captains were encouraged to organise games of cricket, handball or football, leapfrog, quoits, vaulting, running 'in short at all manly and healthy exercises'. Equally, given the role of the rifleman, swimming and learning to swim was recommended, as was regular bathing for hygiene purposes.

Finally, Stewart's *Regulations* also prescribed both the officers and other ranks' uniform and equipment. As the text of this section revealed, Hessian *Jäger* and the existing fifth rifle battalions of the 60th were very much the model, deep green being selected for the corps uniforms and most of their equipment and black leather belts equally deriving from that source. Stewart, in respect of the Rifleman's uniform, stressed the crucial links between personal hygiene, a smart appearance and morale. 'In the soldier's dressing well and with smartness the principal object is first cleanliness (and cleanliness is at all times health) and afterwards a certain degree of self-pride which being well-dressed gives every Soldier, and which self-pride should be encouraged, for it will in the end make him a better man.'

Stewart, though, was not alone in shaping the nuts and bolts of the men at Blatchington. Colonel Manningham found sufficient time to escape his duties at Court during the spring of 1803 to visit his Rifle Corps. Manningham made a critical contribution to both the 95th and the operational role of light infantry in general by composing a series of four lectures. These focused on the practical aspects of carrying out reconnaissance by patrols, establishing piquets, the conduct of vanguards and rearguards and various general issues such as infiltration tactics and marksmanship. Whilst much of the material Manningham covered was contained in the earlier work of various German authors, he notably provided a succinct blueprint for the operation of light infantry in the field, enlightened by his own combat experience.

Though still not officially a regiment, Stewart's men soon attracted attention. No less a person than Vice-Admiral Horatio Nelson specifically requested that a contingent of Stewart's Riflemen be attached to his command for the raid on Copenhagen. Thus a company of Stewart's men commanded by Captain Thomas Sidney Beckwith embarked on board Nelson's flagship, HMS *Elephant*. At the Battle of Copenhagen, on 2 April 1802, whilst Stewart was aboard the *Elephant*, the remainder of the detachment were dispersed throughout the fleet where their services as sharpshooters were appreciated. Embodying the spirit of the corps, the officers did all they could to assist in the fighting of the ships, the regiment's Adjutant, Lieutenant Grant, having the dubious distinction of having his head taken off by a cannon-ball whilst helping to serve the guns on HMS *Isis*.

Whether or not it was just coincidence, shortly after the unit's return on 18 January 1803, the Rifle Corps was ordered to be placed among the numbered regiments of the line, titled 'the 95th or Rifle Regiment'. Whilst Stewart was Colonel, Beckwith (only recently promoted to Major) was appointed its Lieutenant-Colonel, an officer who was to become the regiment's much-admired commander in the Peninsula. As a permanent regiment on the British Establishment and less likely to suffer an arbitrary dissolution, it was decided that the various documents that had guided their training needed to be brought together. Thus both Stewart's *Regulations* and Manningham's lectures were combined in a single document that became the 95th's point of reference, *The Green Book*.

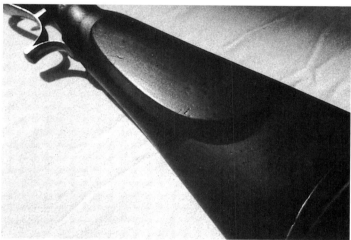

Top, this is a close-up of the distinctive ring neck cock and flat lock mechanism of the Baker. Just forward of the frizzen is the simple iron sight with which most were fitted. *Tim Edwards Collection.* *Middle,* here the raised cheek comb on the left of the stock is clearly visible, as is the scroll-shaped trigger guard. The raised comb was a common feature on most styles of rifle as it helped bring the eye of the shooter directly behind the sights. It has a slight upward angle to help direct the recoil squarely onto the shoulder. *Tim Edwards Collection.* *Bottom,* the open lid of the brass patch box reveals the small receptacle in which greased patches, spare flints and the like were stored. Earlier versions of the Baker had larger and more elaborate boxes, with separate compartments for each item. *Tim Edwards Collection.*

BAKER RIFLE

By 1800 it had been recognised that neither the existing British-made rifled muskets were suitable nor could German sources be relied upon. The exact series of events that led the Board of Ordnance to commission the Whitechapel gunmaker Ezekiel Baker to produce his rifle is unclear, although the fact Baker was a close friend of the Prince of Wales could not have hurt. It appears the Board invited various leading gunmakers to a trial of their various rifles at Woolwich on 4 February 1800. Whilst there is no official record of this competitive test (only Baker's own uncorroborated account published two years later in his *Remarks on Rifle Guns*), in March 1800 the Board gave Baker an order for a number of pattern rifles and barrels so they could assess various designs and calibres. From Baker's subsequent comments, Manningham was closely involved in the rapid decision-making process that made the final selection.

Baker's initial presentation of rifles followed the same dimensions as a standard infantry musket and were immediately rejected by Manningham as being far too heavy due to the thick barrel. Rather, Manningham provided Baker with a German *Jäger* rifle and essentially directed him to copy it. Having thus focused on the familiar *Jäger* style of rifle with a barrel length of 30 inches, the next issue was calibre. Baker had manufactured some that were of the standard .75 for a musket, with eight deep-cut grooves and others down to .625 with seven grooves. As with the process leading to the first order, there is a lack of hard evidence as to the testing process and discussions that must have occurred. The rifle with the standard .75 calibre of the Brown Bess musket, intended to enable Riflemen to use the same ammunition as the line infantry, was immediately rejected. Instead, the smaller .625 calibre 'carbine-bore' version found favour, with the seven square grooves making one complete turn in 10 feet (a quarter of a turn in a 30-inch barrel). Thus the first batch of 800 were ordered before the end of March from various gunmakers in London and Birmingham specifically for the 95th.

This first model of the Baker rifle had the established *Jäger* 30-inch barrel with a simple folding backsight. It had the standard large lock mechanism (some six and a half inches in length), with a swan neck cock as fitted to the Brown Bess musket. Like German *Jäger* rifles, it had a scrolled brass trigger guard to help ensure a firm grip and, on the left of the butt, there was a raised cheek-rest for additional support when aiming. Like most rifles, it had a 'butt-trap' or patchbox of around six inches in length where greased linen patches and tools were stored. The lid of the patchbox was made of brass and was hinged at the rear to allow it to be flipped up to gain access. The rifle's overall length was 45 and three-quarter inches and had a total weight of just under 9lbs.

Again following the German style, Baker's rifle was designed to take a long 24 inch bladed sword bayonet that could be clipped on to a metal bar attached just behind the muzzle. Although the long and heavy sword bayonet made the weapon very awkward to manage, two facts must be borne in mind. Firstly, given the rifle was 13 to 20 inches shorter than the standard infantry muskets, if the Rifleman was ever to engage in a bayonet fight, this additional length was vital. Secondly, it was a weapon that was only to be used as a last resort – Riflemen by definition were sharpshooters.

It must be stressed that Baker's rifle was not designed as a hunting weapon, but rather a mass-produced military weapon that was 'soldier-proof'. It took an already established military calibre ball, had a reasonable rate of fire and was to prove generally accurate on a battlefield at ranges up to 150 yards. It was also sufficiently robust to take a bayonet and withstand the rigours of hand-to-hand combat during a lengthy period of service.

This compared to the graceful custom-built American Long Rifle, that, while lighter, more accurate and more economic in its consumption of powder and ball, was more difficult to load and maintain, easily broken and could not take a bayonet.

As with any new weapon, particularly one that became fashionable, there were soon modifications and effectively new models. A lighter 'carbine' version for the cavalry was almost immediately approved, being otherwise identical. Various of the fashionable Volunteer Associations ordered their own, those made for the Duke of Cumberland's Corps of Sharp Shooters in August 1803 having a barrel 33 inches in length.

As the war progressed, there were also changes to the standard Baker. What might loosely be termed a 'second' pattern was fitted with a 'Newland' lock that had a flat-faced ring neck cock. In 1806 a 'third' pattern was introduced that included a pistol grip trigger guard and smaller four and a half-inch patchbox with a plain rounded front. The lock plate was flat, five inches in length with a steeped down tail, raised semi-water proof pan, a flat ring neck cock and was fitted with a sliding safety-bolt. With the arrival of the New Land Pattern of Brown Bess musket around 1810, with its flat lock and ring-necked cock, the Baker's lock followed suit with what was effectively a 'fourth' pattern. It also had a 'slit-stock', a slot in the underpart of the stock about five sixteenth of an inch wide. This modification was made by Ezekiel Baker after receiving reports of the jamming of rifle ramrods in the rifle stock due to the accumulation of dirt in the base of the ramrod channel or the swelling of the wood when wet.

Not all rifles being manufactured for the British Army were Baker's. The original carbine version proved too long for convenience for mounted troops and so, during the summers of 1803 and 1805, there was a further set of trials of various shorter models. This time Baker faced serious competition from other well-known gunmakers such as Henry Nock, Arnold, Thomas Gill and Durs Egg, particularly as Baker chose to move away from the tried and tested quarter-turn rifling over the length of the barrel to an increased half-turn. Consequently the Board of Ordnance chose Egg's rifled carbine with a quarter-turn rifling down the length of its 20-inch barrel for the cavalry.

The demand for the standard Baker rifle continued to grow well beyond the initial 800 ordered for the single battalion of the 95th. Soon the fifth battalion 60th was re-equipped, and by 1810 sufficient Baker rifles had to be procured for an additional two battalions each of the 60th and 95th, as well as various components of the King's German Legion, other German units such as the Brunswick *Oels* and the Portuguese *Caçadores*. Those required by the regular army were in addition to numerous volunteer formations that chose to constitute themselves as rifle corps, and the East India Company ordered its first consignment in 1802. On average over 2000 rifles a year of the various types were being completed in Birmingham and London workshops between 1804-15. The figures for Birmingham alone show that between those dates a total of 14,695 rifles were completed, along with 32,582 rifle barrels and 37,338 rifle locks. Ultimately there were too many and there were serious storage problems at the Tower. One consequence of this was that in 1810 the Shropshire Militia were issued with Baker's, followed by the Pembroke and Caernavon Militia in 1811 and 1812 respectively, just to help ease the storage issue.

LIGHT BRIGADE

It is appropriate to return to the Duke of York's idea of training whole regiments as light infantry which was first proposed in 1801. At long last, the detrimental practice, albeit a necessity at the time, of detaching light companies from their parent

Sir John Moore was amongst the most gifted generals in the British Army and his training and leadership of the regiments at Shorncliffe ensured that Wellington had in the Peninsula the finest body of light infantry and Riflemen in the world at his disposal.

regiments had been recognised. Hence in 1803, the Duke ordered that two entire regiments be so trained, that never again would commanders on campaign have to pillage the light infantry companies of the battalions to field coherent bodies of light infantry. It also made sense to include the recently established regiment of Riflemen, who, it was reasonably assumed, would operate in conjunction with these regiments of light infantry. Thus, in January 1803, the 52nd Foot was re-designated as light infantry, followed by the 43rd Foot in July. That same month the 43rd received their new designation and began their conversion, and the 52nd and 95th Rifles were ordered to assemble at the Shorncliffe Army camp near Folkestone under the command of Major-General John Moore. Meanwhile the 43rd took almost a full year to complete its transformation and thus did not arrive until June 1804.

Moore was a logical choice given his extensive service with light troops. The son of a Glasgow doctor, Moore, born 30 November 1761, first entered the British Army in 1776. He subsequently saw considerable active service in North America, Corsica, the Caribbean and Ireland, much of it with light troops of one type or another. Having first cut his teeth in the forests of North America, the young Major Moore spent 1788-90 attached to the 60th Royal Americans, helping train two new battalions. Having commanded the 51st Foot in the Mediterranean during the opening stages of the French wars, in 1796 he was dispatched to St Lucia with the local rank of brigadier-general. Here the fighting found him leading various companies of light infantry and detachments of German light troops such as Lowenstein's through the hills and jungles of the island in what was effectively guerrilla warfare. Consequently, by 1798 Moore was identified as a natural commander of light troops and when dispatched to Ireland during the rebellion of 1798, he was given command of a 'Light Brigade' of some 2,000 men.

This Light Brigade consisted of the four companies of the fifth battalion 60th *'Jägers'*, a Light Infantry battalion of Irish Militia, a 50-strong troop of Hompesch's Mounted Riflemen and a battery of six guns. It was at the head of his light brigade that on 20 June 1798 he fought a classic light infantry action near Foulke's Mill in Wexford against a force of Irish insurgents some five times the size of his own that he displayed all the elements that would later become familiar in the Peninsular. Moving up the road towards the enemy, the Riflemen of the 60th deployed as an advanced skirmish line, supported by two formed companies of Irish militia on both sides of the road, along with his guns and *hussars*. The ensuing action proved confusing, some of the militia required Moore's personal leadership to prevent them running. However, after a hard fight through the surrounding woods, the enemy was completely defeated. Given that his Irish militia had proved somewhat prone to panic in the dispersed and confused combat, Moore subsequently devised a simple 16-page set of instructions of light infantry drills and evolutions for them. This short document reflected the now generally accepted orthodoxy that any body of light troops ought to contain a combination of Riflemen and conventionally armed light infantry.

Having been promoted Major-General in July 1798 and participating in the brief and ill-fated Helder campaign, Moore was ordered to Egypt. On his way he was ordered to inspect various British regiments stationed on Minorca, including a relatively new corps specifically raised as light infantry, the 90th Foot. The 90th had been trained in Rottenberg's *Regulations* whilst stationed in Portugal by another leading exponent of light infantry, General Sir Charles Stuart. Although Moore had actually commanded Rottenberg's four companies of riflemen in Ireland, he had not had the opportunity to see an entire regiment of light infantry utilising his *Regulations*. It is recorded that Moore was suitably impressed when observing the 90th drilling on the glacis of Fort St Philip. After distinguished service in Egypt, which included the 90th as part of his command, Moore proceeded to Shorncliffe.

Whilst the Shorncliffe episode is often quoted as a defining moment in the evolution of British light troops, this is to overplay wildly its significance. There is no doubt that Moore was a gifted officer who may well have rivalled Wellington if he had not been mortally wounded at Corunna in January 1809. Moore himself, however, fully acknowledged he was no innovator and young officers who had an opportunity to visit Moore's extensive library identified on his shelves the works of various German authors on light infantry including Ewald and Rottenberg. The drill and manoeuvres he taught the battalions of the 43rd and 52nd had been the standard for all light companies in the British Army for nearly five years and he later commented that he made 'de Rottenburg the groundwork…it only requires to be properly applied'. Thus, other than a few minor changes derived from practical application, Rottenberg's work was adhered to in its entirety. It should, though, be stressed that Moore also taught Dundas's *Rules and Regulations* so as to enable the 43rd and 52nd to fight in rigid linear formation alongside line infantry if required.

Another German author that influenced Moore was Lieutenant-General Andrew Emmerich, an officer of Brunswick *Jäger* who had served in both the Seven Years War and the American War of Independence. Reflecting the shared German military ethos of Emmerich, Ewald and Rottenberg, Moore stressed the need for officers to lead by example and to develop a close personal knowledge of the character and abilities of each and every man under their command. Officers needed to maintain the closest of holds on their men, given the dispersed nature of their deployment, particularly in open country where light infantry was highly vulnerable to enemy cavalry. Echoing Stewart's Company System, Moore required regimental commanders to delegate power to captains in respect of punishments, rewards, drill, food and clothing, and demanded all officers treat their men kindly and maintain their temper at all times. Equally, following the recommendations of Emmerich, Rottenberg and German authors in general, even junior NCOs were allocated far greater responsibilities and expected to take the initiative to a much greater extent than would be the norm in a standard British infantry regiment. For example, Moore taught that reconnaissance patrols should consist of a corporal and four privates, the junior NCO being capable of sketching maps and interrogating locals.

Having overseen the 43rd and 52nd being trained as light infantry, Shorncliffe for Moore functioned as a standard brigade training camp where the British Army's specialist light infantry learnt to operate together. The 95th had already been fully trained by Stewart as Riflemen (Stewart was promoted to Brigadier-General in early 1804, his place at the head of the 95th being taken by Lieutenant-Colonel Thomas Beckwith). At Shorncliffe they learned how to operate in conjunction with the regiments of light infantry, once these had been fully trained to the same standard as the 95th.

Although Moore finished training the 43rd, 52nd and 95th in September 1805, four further battalions were trained in a similar manner as a 'light brigade' on the Curragh of Kildare in Ireland in May 1808 by Rottenberg himself. Later, Rottenberg returned to England and, at Brabourn Lees barracks in Ashford, trained the 68th, 85th and 71st as light infantry to help meet the demand for such troops in the Peninsular. Meanwhile, for the three regiments that had trained together at Shorncliffe they were soon to be given an opportunity to test their skills for real.

RIFLEMAN ON CAMPAIGN

BECOMING A RIFLEMAN

Whilst the 95th began as a select body of soldiers from which any doubtful characters were weeded out, the inevitable shrinkage due to illness, accidents and combat meant the regiment soon had to recruit like any normal British formation. Despite raising a second battalion in 1805 and a third in 1809, the 95th did not maintain a home battalion for recruitment purposes. This meant that each battalion often had to struggle just to maintain an average of six companies in the field at any one time, and a considerable body of officers and NCOs were detached for long periods on recruitment duties. Nevertheless, the Rifles were successful beyond all comparison in recruiting, their dashing uniform and reputation managing to attract even serving soldiers who volunteered from existing units.

Benjamin Harris, who had originally been drafted from the Army of the Reserve in 1802 into the 66th Foot, had already, given his short stature, been posted to its light company. Five years later, in 1807, whilst in Dublin with the 66th's light company: 'I one day saw a corps of the 95th Rifles, and fell in love with their smart, dashing, and devil-may-care appearance, that nothing would serve me till I was a Rifleman myself'. Shortly afterwards, having arrived at Cashal, Harris volunteered into its second battalion at the Royal Oak Inn, along with men from the Irish Militia whom he felt 'were as reckless and devil-may-care a set of men as ever I beheld, either before or since'.

The flow of volunteers from serving units was, however, far from sufficient, hence the age-old method of 'beating up' for recruits became a familiar duty for many officers and men of the 95th. As with the rest of the British Army, the most valuable source of new Riflemen, since they had already received basic training, was the continuous flow of militiamen, both rankers and officers, encouraged to 'volunteer' by recruiting parties. Indeed it was just such a group that Harris had

fallen in with in 1807 and it is possible another well-known diarist from the regiment was amongst them. Edward Costello, a young Irishman from Dublin, relates how, having first volunteered into the Dublin Militia in June 1806, late the following year 'our regiment was stationed at Londonderry... where I volunteered into the 95th'.

Harris was far from unique; almost every Rifleman who has left an account of his time in the 95th was originally a militiaman. William Surtees, who ultimately became Quartermaster of the third battalion 95th, began his military service at the tender age of 17 in the Northumberland Militia. He soon volunteered into the 56th Foot, seeing active service in Holland in 1799, and was then posted to Cork, where he came across an officer and soldiers of what was then the Experimental Rifle Corps. As Surtees relates: 'I cannot account for the impulse with which I was urged on, from the moment I had seen one of the men, to enter this corps. Something strange seemed to push me on'. According to Surtees, the attraction of the 95th was such that even unemployed officers volunteered into its ranks as privates. 'About this period we had several individuals serving in the corps as soldiers, who had been officers in the army during the late war, but who, from different causes, had been reduced to the necessity of enlisting as private soldiers'.

Surtees went on to identify four such examples personally known to himself. Two had held rank in the militia: Conway Welch, who had been the Adjutant of the Surrey Rangers, and a 'Tait', who had been a captain in the Caithness Legion. Two had held rank on the Regular Establishment: a 'Hughes' who had been a lieutenant in the line and a 'McLaughlan' who had been an officer in the light company of the 35th Foot. The former, having quickly gained the rank of corporal and then secretary to the colonel, was fortunate shortly to be recalled to his commissioned rank at full-pay. The latter, due to what Surtees termed

'dissipated habits', had in fact twice held commissioned rank but twice been obliged to sell out for gambling debts.

Later in the war, particularly after the terrible losses on the Corunna campaign, Harris, amongst 'the strongest and smartest of our men', was selected to join a recruiting party. As was typical, a junior officer, Lieutenant Pratt, seconded by a prime example of the senior British NCO, Sergeant-Major Adams, led Harris' party. Along with another Rifleman, William Brotherwood, the four-strong party set out for Hastings. Hearing that the East Kent Militia were at Lydd, Harris and Adams 'stopped there about an hour to display ourselves before them, and try if we could coax a few of them into the Rifles. We strutted up and down before their ranks arm in arm, and made no small sensation amongst them. When on the recruiting service in those days, men were accustomed to make as gallant a show as they could, and accordingly we had both smartened ourselves up a trifle. The sergeant-major was quite a beau in his way; he had a sling belt to his sword like a field-officer, a tremendous green feather in his cap, a flaring sash, his whistle and powder flask displayed, an officer's pelisse over one shoulder, and a double allowance of ribbons in his cap; whilst I myself was also as smart as I dared appear, with my rifle slung at my shoulder. In this guise we made as much of ourselves as if we had both been generals, and, as I said, created quite a sensation, the militiamen cheering us as we passed up and down... we persuaded many men, during the hour we figured before them, that the Rifles were the only boys fit for them to join'.

This, though, was only the beginning of Harris and Adams' efforts as they completed their journey to Hastings, where men of the Leicester Militia were being 'volunteered'. On arrival, they were dismayed to discover a recruiting party of the 7th Foot had already succeeded in convincing 125 rankers and two officers to don red coats, but displaying the

initiative and fortitude characteristic of Riflemen, they both set to work. 'The appearance of our Rifle uniform, and a little of Sergeant Adams' blarney, so took the fancies of the volunteers, that we got everyone of them for the Rifle Corps, and both officers into the bargain'. Despite this, it was hard work and, as Harris comments, very familiar methods of inducement were resorted to as 'for three days and nights we kept up the dance and the drunken riot'. Later, after a cursory medical examination, they were attested and marched off to the regiment, having each received 10 guineas bounty (which, apart from the two guineas held back to pay for 'necessaries', they mostly spent on drink).

As Wellington settled into the long series of campaigns in the Peninsular, the militia continued to provide most of the numbers required to maintain the battalions serving in the field. Indeed, when the third battalion was formed at Ashford, Kent in April 1809, the continuing popularity of the Rifles ensured 1,100 volunteers from the militia came forward within three days. According to Costello, militiamen from the light companies were preferred. 'Our regiment was shortly afterwards raised to one thousand strong, chiefly through volunteers from the militia, our common medium of supply at the time. In the knowledge and

Despite their reputation for travelling light, even the 60th and 95th Rifles relied on cumbersome wagons to transport much of their equipment.

Opposite, camp scenes such as this only became possible from January 1813 onwards when tents became common issue. Prior to this, barns, houses or quickly erected blankets thrown over branches had to suffice for cover in the field.

exercise of their military duties during the war, the militia regiments were almost as good as the troops of the line, and the men who joined our battalion – chiefly the élite of the light companies of the different corps – were, in general, a fine set of young fellows.'

The new recruits were first marched to the regiment's barracks. The 95th was firstly based at barracks at Hythe in Kent, then later moved to Brabourne Lees near Ashford before ending up at Shorncliffe. There, even if he had been in the militia, the recruit received an intense period of training prior to being despatched to his allocated battalion. During this time the everyday life of a Rifleman had much in common with the rest of the Army.

The new Riflemen were luckier in some respects than earlier generations of British soldiers in that rather than being billeted on unwilling innkeepers and civilians, the 1790s had seen a vast expenditure on purpose-built barracks. It ought to be stressed that the reasons for this move were unconnected with the welfare of the soldier. Rather it was a combination of the Home Office's desire to concentrate troops in urban areas for police duties, whilst isolating them from any subversive notions emanating from the civilian population. This explain why, whilst it helped build an *esprit de corps*, the barracks of the age were often poorly built, the common soldier being allocated less room than was normally given to a convict! The inevitable overcrowding ensured that issues of sanitation were ignored and it was normal practice for soldiers to have to share beds, privacy being unknown.

At least on home service, the Rifleman was paid his daily subsistence money directly, choosing how they purchased food and how it was cooked. This subsistence money provided three basic meals a day to men who, in their previous civilian life, had often not known from one day to the next when, or if, they would eat. As there was no such post as 'cook', soldiers traditionally took it in turns to prepare meals. James Anton, Quartermaster of the 42nd Foot, commented that the soldiers were 'perfectly contented' with this set-up. 'We breakfasted about nine in the morning, on bread and milk; dined about two in the afternoon, on potatoes and a couple of salt herrings, boiled in the pot with the potatoes; a bottle of small beer and a slice of bread served for supper, when we were disposed to take that meal, which soldiers seldom do. On the whole, I am certain our expenses for messing, dear as markets were, did not exceed three shillings and sixpence each, weekly.' If the Rifleman wanted anything in addition to this feast, he had to purchase it from what few pennies were left from his pay of a shilling a day after the normal deductions: subsistence (for the above basic food stuffs) and 'Off-Reckonings' (the age-old practice of deducting a few pence per day from the soldier's pay to cover the cost of his clothing).

This recreated veteran reflects far more accurately the general appearance of the average Rifleman of the 95th after years of campaigning in the heat and dust of Spain.
English Heritage

The neat and tidy appearance of these recreated Riflemen suggests they are mostly new recruits.
English Heritage

ON CAMPAIGN

In Britain, purpose-built barracks and money for subsistence was the norm, but on campaign it was all very different. Whilst tents were available, Wellington felt they were an encumbrance in the field and few were issued until early 1813. Thus all too often the Rifleman, along with the rest of the Army, had but the stars for a roof. If it was possible, branches and undergrowth was fashioned into a rough billet, while any barn or house was soon occupied, albeit officers having first call on such. Sometimes tents were improvised by Riflemen, who stitched loops to the covers of their blankets (each soldier had one). Two blankets were then looped together and stands of rifles used at either end to serve as tent poles. Four men would huddle under this scanty cover, sharing the remaining two blankets for warmth.

With food, the situation was also very different in the field. Here there was a daily issue of rations rather than the payment of subsistence, the stipulated daily ration being neither generous in quantity, nor an example of variety. It consisted of one pound of bread or one and a half pounds of flour, a pound of beef or half a pound of pork (including bone!), a small quantity of peas, butter, cheese, rice and a quart of beer (a pint of wine or one-third pint of rum could be substituted). Each four-man mess would share a camp-kettle into which they placed all the foodstuffs provided, along with the necessary amount of water. This ensured the boiled beef or pork yielded an additional pint of broth and that the staple meal was a mixed stew of almost every item. Apart from practicality, this made some sense when it is appreciated that the 'bread' issued was in fact a form of hard-tack biscuit renowned to be hard enough to deflect a musket ball. Breaking up such rock-hard items and soaking them in a stew was almost the only way they could be consumed without breaking teeth.

In practice the inevitable logistical problems of ensuring the daily arrival of supplies often meant soldiers went hungry. On the gruelling retreat from Burgos in November 1812, logistics collapsed, the consequences being sardonically recalled in the renowned memoirs of Sir John Kincaid: 'There was plenty of water to apologise for the want of better fluids, but bread sent no apology at all'. Kincaid went on to reminisce that care had to be taken when sampling another soldier's meal: 'While I was toasting myself at his [General Alten's] fire, so sharply set that I could have eaten one of my boots, I observed his German orderly dragoon, at an adjoining fire, stirring up the contents of a camp-kettle, that once more revived my departing hopes, and I presently had the satisfaction of seeing him dipping in some basins, presenting one to the general, one to the aide-de-camp, and a third to myself. The mess which it contained I found, after swallowing the whole at a draught, was neither more nor less than the produce of a piece of beef boiled in plain water; and, though it would have been enough to have physicked a dromedary at any other time, yet, as I could then have made a good hole in the dromedary himself, it sufficiently satisfied my cravings to make me equal to anything for the remainder of the day.'

Sergeant Cooper of the 7th Foot summed it up when he wrote 'when a man entered upon a soldier's life...he should have parted with half his

Although soldiers often wrote of the heavy burden they bore, there was little that was not essential. These various items include many carried in the backpack: an open tinder box for lighting fires sits next to a tin cup, whilst the inclusion of a toothbrush and soap box may surprise many.

stomach'. Whilst Kincaid's anecdote of the retreat from Burgos referred to a particularly extreme occurrence, Cooper summed up the average situation when he went on to say that commonly 'we were reduced to half rations, and once, for a whole week, we had nothing but one pound of bad beef daily. When bread could not be obtained, we got a pint of unground wheat, or a sheaf of wheat out of the fields, or else two pounds of potatoes'.

Attempts to remedy this situation from local sources, such as farmers and innkeepers, usually went for nought: either the commissariat had not the funds to purchase food in bulk or the local suppliers sought the highest prices for the least quantity. Given Wellington's strictures against looting, there were limits to the amount of food that could be foraged even when the Army was advancing into enemy territory. George Wood of the 82nd Foot commented that, during four days in the Pyrenees in 1813, the regiment had nothing but the leaves on the trees to sustain them 'which we chewed as we passed along to assuage the craving of hunger'.

STANDING IN RAGS

Whilst the smart green uniform of the Rifleman did wonders for recruitment back in Britain, on campaign it rapidly deteriorated. Officially each Rifleman was designated to receive a complete suit of clothing each year to replace worn-out items (the cost of which continued to be deducted from his pay as Off-Reckonings). Like their rations, however, all too often replacement clothing and equipment were late or failed to arrive at all, leaving the Rifleman to scavenge what he could locally. Whilst marching back and forth across the often impoverished and barren landscape of Portugal and Spain offered scant pickings, the successful storming of a French-held town or city provided irresistible temptations, none more dramatic than Ciudad Rodrigo in January 1812.

Kincaid memorably recounted the 95th's appearance as it marched out of the captured town the following day. 'Lord Wellington happened to be riding in at the gate at the time that we were marching out, and had the curiosity to ask the officer of the leading company, what regiment it was, for there was scarcely a vestige of uniform among the men, some of whom were dressed in Frenchmen's coats, some in white breeches, and huge jack-boots, some with cocked hats and queues; most of their swords were fixed on the rifles, and stuck full of hams, tongues, and loaves of bread, and not a few were carrying bird-cages! There never was a better masked corps!' This description is confirmed by Costello who wrote:

'The next morning, we marched over the bridge dressed in all variety of clothes imaginable. Some had jack-boots on, others wore frock-coats, or had epaulettes, and some even had monkeys on their shoulders...I was afterwards told by several of our men that the Duke of Wellington, who saw us on our march, inquired of his staff: "Who the devil are those fellows?"'.

As ever, the confusion and traumas of a headlong retreat ensured the average Rifleman was left standing in little more than rags. Whilst Moore led the bulk of the Army to Corunna, General Craufurd took the Light Brigade to Vigo from where they were evacuated. After the voyage home, having suffered several days of violent storms and not having eaten for two days, Harris related how the emaciated soldiers had to endure their troopship spending a further six days standing off Spithead before being allowed to disembark. 'The inhabitants flocked down to the beach to see us as we did so, and they must have been a good deal surprised at the spectacle we presented. Our beards were long and ragged; almost all were without shoes and stockings; many had their clothes and accoutrements in fragments, with their heads swathed in old rags, and our weapons were covered with rust; whilst not a few had now, from toil and fatigue, become quite blind.'

Despite Manningham's recommendation that Riflemen should carry as little baggage as possible, like infantry throughout the Army, their backpacks were loaded with anything up to 60lbs of equipment. It was even worse for some; Harris as a skilled cobbler was obliged to carry, in addition to the standard load of 60lbs, an extra load of tools. 'For my own part, being a handicraft, I marched under a weight sufficient to impede the free motions of a donkey; for besides my well-filled kit [knapsack], there was the greatcoat rolled on its top, my blanket and camp kettle, my haversack, stuffed full of leather for repairing the men's shoes, together with a hammer and other tools

(the lapstone I took the liberty of flinging to the devil), ship-biscuit and beef for three days. I also carried my canteen filled with water, my hatchet and rifle, and eighty rounds of ball cartridge in my pouch.'

An exhausting burden at the best of times, on the retreat to Vigo it was fatal. 'Our knapsacks, too, were a bitter enemy on this prolonged march. Many a man died, I am convinced, who would have borne up well to the end of the retreat but for the infernal load we carried on our backs. My own knapsack was my bitterest enemy; I felt it press me to the earth almost at times, and more than once felt as if I should die under its deadly embrace. The knapsack, in my opinion, should have been abandoned at the very commencement of the retrograde movement, as it would have been better to have lost them altogether, if, by such loss, we could have saved the poor fellows who, as it was, died strapped to them on the road.'

As Harris further relates, the condition of his company's leatherwork ensured there was no shortage of work. 'The shoes and boots of our party were now mostly either destroyed or useless to us, from foul roads and long miles, and many of the men were entirely barefooted, with knapsacks and accoutrements altogether in a dilapidated state.' This ensured that, for Harris at least, there was a

Despite the difficulties, many babies were born to women accompanying the regiment. Rifleman Harris recounted harrowing stories involving these women and young children on the gruelling retreat to Corunna.

Opposite, although often overlooked, the Rifles included their fair share of women and children on campaign. Whether struggling through rivers or over mountains, come rain or shine, many coped as well, if not better, than their menfolk with the hardships of campaign.

bright side, for during this gruelling retreat, Harris' cobbling skills were indispensable to the continued effectiveness of his company and his officers did their utmost to keep him out of the firing line.

Harris, however, along with the other skilled artisans in the regiment paid for this in another way, given they were expected to be available day and night to employ their respective trades. Harris tells how, at the end of yet another day's long and gruelling march, having found a comfortable refuge in a convent, he was roused late at night by his battalion Quartermaster, none other than William Surtees. Along with the battalion's other cobblers, Harris was required at General Craufurd's order to sew up barrels of gunpowder in leather hides by candlelight. Surtees withdrew, leaving the bleary-eyed Harris to motivate his somewhat disgruntled band in what was a far from risk-free task. 'The Riflemen were wearied, unwilling, and out of temper; and it was as much as I could do to get them to assist me. Moreover, they were so reckless that they seemed rather to wish to blow the convent into the air than to get on with their work. One moment the candle was dropped, and nearly extinguished; the next they lost their implements between the rafters of the floor, flaring the light about amongst the barrels; and wishing, as I remonstrated with them, that the powder might ignite, and blow me, themselves, and the general to...'

At least Harris, on this occasion, had the benefit of a roof over his head. When the 95th were performing their role as part of the rearguard, they had to contend with far worse. The long retreat from Burgos, through Madrid and almost back to the Portuguese frontier in November 1812, made memories of the retreat under Moore in 1808 seem almost pleasant; then, at least, the roads through the mountains were frozen solid. In 1812, the soldiers had to contend with the daily misery of rain and mud. As Costello recounts: 'The rain fell in torrents,

and the roads were so heavy--one or two feet deep in mud in many places--most of our men lost their shoes, and were obliged to march barefooted. Unfortunately, I was one of them...When we reached our halting-ground for the night, our prospect was most desolate for we were wet to the skin, and without fire or shelter. The first thing I did was take off my jacket and shirt and wring out about half a gallon of water. I placed them upon my back to dry as they might. Most of our men cut down boughs of trees to keep themselves out of the mud, but it was some hours before we could obtain that greatest of luxuries, a good fire. It had been a fatiguing day, and although possessed of a ravenous appetite, we had nothing to satisfy it. We had not a morsel to eat, no rations having been issued, so our men suffered from pangs of cold, and hunger.'

Kincaid confirms this description with his usual hint of irony. 'We were now walking nearly knee deep, in a stiff mud, into which no man could thrust his foot with the certainty of having a shoe at the end of it when he pulled it out again. And that we might not be miserable by halves, we had this evening to regale our chops with the last morsel of biscuit that they were destined to grind during the retreat...We cut down some boughs of trees to keep us out of the mud, and lay down to sleep on them, wet to the skin; but the cannonade of the afternoon had been succeeded after dark by a continued firing of musketry, which led us to believe that our pickets were attacked, and in momentary expectation of an order to stand to our arms, we kept ourselves awake the whole night. We were not a little provoked when we found, next morning, that it had been occasioned by numerous stragglers from the different regiments, shooting at the pigs belonging to the peasantry, which were grazing in the wood.' As Simmons recorded, at the conclusion of the retreat at Ciudad Rodrigo the officers were in as bad a state as their men. 'Most of us walking barefooted, my shoes also

Left, like their men, the officers' uniform of the 95th had undergone several changes by 1806. Whilst the barrel sash had become the norm, the most notable change was the disappearance of the heavy Tarleton helmet and its replacement by a conical shako similar to that worn by the common Rifleman.

Opposite, Captain Kent, his uniform reflecting the strong light cavalry influence on the clothes and equipment of 95th officers. Apart from the obvious pelisse and curved sabre, his cavalry-style overalls are even reinforced with leather insets. As can be seen with his shako, the officers' version could be worn with its peak turned up.

having no bottoms, as well as my friends'. My legs and feet much frost-bitten, so could hardly crawl.'

The constant stress and trauma of these conditions produced in the minds of the soldiers something akin to what today we might term post traumatic stress syndrome. According to Costello: 'Hunger, incessant duty, and fatigue were the disagreeable things attendant upon our life in the Peninsula, and I am convinced that it was these sufferings that so often rendered our men callous to death. At different periods during the war, some men, from the privations they endured, wished to be shot, and exposed themselves in action for that purpose'.

This close-up of a recreated officers' shako illustrates the leather peak that was commonly worn up. Otherwise the officers' shako was identical in shape and dimensions to the other ranks', albeit made from far finer quality materials and finished to a noticeably higher standard of construction.
English Heritage

The suffering endured by Wellington's men during the gruelling retreat of November 1812 ensured the belated issue of new and improved camping equipment. By the commencement of the 1813 campaign, Surtees recorded that '…each company received four tents, thus allowing about 20 men for each. The officers of each company had one among them, and the field and staff officers in like proportion. These were carried on mules, which before had carried the camp-kettles; but these being exchanged for smaller ones, the men carried them in turns upon their knapsacks. Thus it rarely happened that the tents were not on the ground nearly as soon as the men…'.

Along with tents, other equipment designed to make life on the march more bearable (and thus hopefully reduce the numbers lost to sickness and invalidity) was issued, including a light tin camp kettle soldiers could carry to replace the previous heavy iron one that had to be transported by mule. To lighten their load, many soldiers chose to dispose of their blankets, particularly as their use as improvised tents was no longer essential. However, the greatcoat was retained, being invaluable when deployed at night on piquet and because it could double as a form of snug sleeping bag. Soldiers relate how they turned the coat upside-down, poking their legs through the sleeves and then buttoning up the front so that the body of the coat wrapped round them.

WOMEN AND CHILDREN

On campaign, many soldiers struck up liaisons, married, and had children. As Harris relates, some even volunteered with a family already in existence, in this case, Rifleman Richard Pullen: 'He brought with him little else to boast of but his wife and his two children, Charles and Susan. Charles was a mischievous boy of about 12, and Susan was a pretty little lass, of about 14 years of age. I remember they all went with us to Copenhagen, and got through that expedition pretty well.'

The Army did not encourage the rank and file to marry in the first place and treated soldiers' wives as an inconvenience at best. In barracks they were permitted the minimum of privacy, often little more than a blanket hung around the bed. The regulations, however, allowed for six women per company to embark on active service with a battalion and these were chosen by lot from among the wives of the soldiers. Thus, like all other regiments in the British Army, the 95th were accompanied on campaign by a number of soldiers' wives, some officially, some not.

The method of selection was at least fair. Common practice was that when a regiment received orders for embarkation, the wives and husbands would gather in each company's respective pay-sergeant's room in the barracks. In order of seniority, sergeants' wives first, then corporals', then privates', each drew from a hat a slip of paper, six of which were marked 'to-go' and the remainder 'not-to-go'. Needless to say, the various soldiers' memoirs of the time abound with heart-breaking stories of the agonising partings just prior to departure of those that were unlucky in this lottery. Those not selected were simply given a cash allowance to return to their home parish, after which the Army considered its duty done.

The justification for embarking any wives at all was not sentimental but rather practical, in that they were expected to assist with cooking, washing, mending clothes and foraging. Kincaid complained that when there were no women with the regiment, 'the ceremony of washing a shirt amounted to a servant's taking it by the collar and giving it a couple of shakes in the water, and then hanging it up to dry'. Fortunately for Kincaid and the rest, the women who accompanied the Army had a reputation for toughness and perseverance, Ensign George Bell of the 34th Foot commenting that they 'stuck to the army like bricks'.

Whilst in the Peninsula, the ranks of many regiments, and certainly those of the 95th, were supplemented by locally recruited Portuguese and Spaniards. Certainly Costello, recording the preparations for embarkation in July 1814 for the return to Britain, commented favourably on such soldiers and was sorry to leave them behind. 'We stopped at a village...where we had to part from our allies, the Spanish and Portuguese. Many deep feelings of regret were felt, particularly by the men of our battalion, on parting with the Spaniards who had been incorporated in our ranks for so long, and who were so distinguished for their gallantry. Sixteen had been drafted into our company, but only five survived to bid us farewell. The poor fellows had grown attached to the battalion and expressed much grief on leaving it... Notwithstanding the wretched and ineffective state of the Spanish armies during the campaigns in the Peninsula, I am convinced, and have indeed become more so from subsequent experience, that the men have the right stuff to make excellent soldiers...'.

OFFICERS AND GENTLEMEN

One of the greatest myths relating to the British Army was that most officers purchased their commissions and were the affluent sons of the land-owning aristocracy. Whilst there was some 10,000 officers in the Army at any given time during the latter part of the Napoleonic Wars, in 1809 only 140 were peers or their sons, and 43 of those were in the Guards. Although there is not the slightest doubt that only those judged to be of a suitable social standing (the contemporary term was 'private gentlemen') usually gained commissions, a considerable proportion of gentlemen gained rank and promotion by means other than their purse.

This was particularly true as the conflict went on--many officers who had originally purchased rank chose to exchange or sell-out at a bargain price to avoid the vagaries and trauma of active service. One estimate suggests that, during the

Amongst the most famous of Rifles officers was Harry Smith. This painting demonstrates how the officers of the Rifles still looked to the light cavalry in fashion, as demonstrated by the fur edged pelisse and braided breeches.

This Rifleman of the North Yorkshire Militia, c.1814, demonstrates how the palm of the right hand was used to exert considerable pressure on the ramrod to seal the patched ball firmly in the breech. An interesting detail is how he has unstrung the cord of his powder flask from his cartridge belt and put it around his neck whilst he has placed the powder flask in a pocket on the left breast of his jacket for ease of access.

Peninsula campaign, less than 20% of first commissions were by purchase and most promotions were by seniority due to vacancies caused by death and injury on active service. This was certainly true of the 95th, few of whose officers had gained their original commissions by purchase and, regardless of their route of entry, all the evidence suggests seniority and merit was the relevant criteria for promotion.

The initial cadre of officers were, like the ranks, those that had been dispatched by their respective regiments to learn how to be Riflemen on the mistaken assumption they would be returning. None, though, seems to have requested to be allowed to return to their original regiment, even when it became obvious the Experimental Rifle Corps was to become an established regiment, this despite some officers having originally purchased into the regiment from which they had been detached. However, there was soon a need for new entrants to the commissioned ranks and, like the rank and file, the militia was a rich source of officers, access being gained by bringing 40 militiamen with them. This was known as 'recruiting for rank', a practice only permitted during wartime. Ultimately 20% of all serving officers had first held a commission in the militia, many of these being the sons of socially humble fathers such as shopkeepers, milliners, doctors and other members of the bourgeoisie.

Possibly the most famous Rifle officer of them all, Kincaid, was just such a 'recruiter'. Originally, he joined his local militia in Glasgow, later becoming an ensign in the North York Militia. In 1809, whilst serving with his regiment in Deal, he, like so many militiamen, was gripped by the irresistible attraction of the 95th. '...any subaltern who could persuade a given number of men to follow him, received a commission in whatever regiment of the line he wished, provided there was a vacancy for himself and followers. I therefore chose that which had long been the object of my secret adoration, as well for its dress as the nature of its services and its achievements, the old ninety-fifth...They had just returned from sharing in the glories and disasters of Sir John Moore's retreat, and were busily employed in organising again for active service. I have never seen a regiment of more gallant bearing than the first battalion there showed itself, from their brilliant chief (the late Sir Sidney Beckwith) downwards; they were all that a soldier could love to look on; and, splendid as was their appearance, it was the least admirable part about them, for the beauty of their system of discipline consisted in their doing everything that was necessary, and nothing that was not, so that every man's duty was a pleasure to him, and the *esprit de corps* was unrivalled.'

Alongside those entering from the militia were some that had enrolled as 'gentlemen volunteers'. These were individuals considered socially suitable to be an officer but who lacked the means or connections to obtain a commission. A commanding officer was at liberty to appoint gentlemen volunteers to accompany the battalion on campaign, who served in the ranks but lived with the officers. Then it was a matter of either waiting for the death of a junior officer to provide an opening or the volunteer participating in a distinguished action, such as membership of a forlorn hope in an assault. They could then hope to be recommended for the vacancy or appointment by distinguished service. The difficulty of treading such a road meant that only 4-5% of commissioned officers gained their rank this way.

As was standard throughout the Army, except for the appointments of quartermaster and paymaster which were traditionally reserved for deserving senior NCOs, the 95th did not commission officers from the ranks other than in exceptional circumstances such as extreme acts of bravery. Even at the height of the Napoleonic Wars, in the British Army as a whole, just 5% were commissioned from the ranks, and such fortunate

individuals usually ended up in regiments posted to undesirable locations such as the fever-ridden Caribbean. Even if they remained in their original regiment, they were soon on the half-pay list. Thus, after Waterloo, one enlisted Rifleman, Dugald Macfarlane of the third battalion 95th Rifles, was commissioned a first lieutenant for distinguished service, 18 July 1815, being placed on the half-pay list in February of the following year.

One of the few possible examples of a serving officer who had originated in the ranks was Costello's commander, Captain Peter O'Hare. Costello relates that O'Hare, a popular officer, 'whose eccentric habits were equalled only by his extremely ugly countenance' was said to have risen from the ranks. True or not, he had joined the Experimental Rifle Corps at its formation in August 1800, transferring from the 69th Foot where he had been a lieutenant since January 1797. Promoted to captain in August 1803, he later rose to the rank of major in the first battalion before being killed leading one of the storming parties during the bloody assault on Badajoz 6 April 1812.

In terms of progression, the Duke of York, who was sympathetic to poor but keen junior officers who could not afford to purchase, maintained a list of meritorious officers to which he referred when opportunities for free promotion occurred. Confidential reports on these officers were maintained and it is known a number of such individuals were appointed, with Colonel Manningham's consent, to the 95th Rifles when it expanded to a second battalion in 1805, and a third in 1809.

The spirit that moved the officers of the Rifles made them a distinct group within the larger family of commissioned ranks in the British Army. Whilst an attachment to a military career and pride in professional accomplishments was common in the British Army, the officers of the Rifles appear to have absorbed the spirit imparted by Stewart and Manningham when the regiment

The horn powder flask was attached to the cartridge box sling by a green worsted cord. The horn was not issued polished, although years of being rubbed by leather and wool on active service might make it so. This one is fitted with an 'English' charger throwing the service charge for the Baker rifle of four and a half drams of powder. The leather cartridge box contained a wooden block drilled out for 50 paper cartridges.
Richard Rutherford-Moore

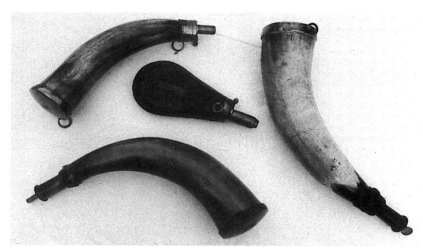

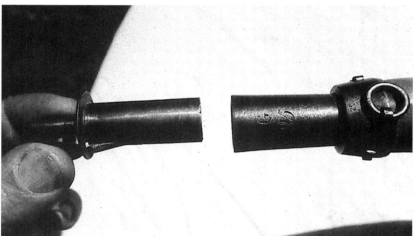

Top, various sizes of horn flask were issued, some of copper. On average they carried just over a pound and a half of gunpowder and were fitted with either an 'English' or 'Irish' charger. **Tim Edwards Collection**

Bottom, Irish chargers such as this were fitted to the earlier horn flasks, but out on campaign these caused problems with the Riflemen losing the detachable 'male' charger, and the female charger also threw roughly the service charge. A cork being inserted into it solved the problem. **Tim Edwards Collection**

was originally raised and firmly maintained by Beckwith. As with so much else, the ethos of the 95th's officers owed much to Rottenberg and the 60th in that the professional attitudes of their German counterparts were conveyed to new officers years later. Kincaid records that 'On my first arrival my whole soul was so absorbed in the interests excited by the service-officers that, for a time, I could attend to nothing else'. From the start, officers were expected not only to learn the various evolutions required of Riflemen, but were expected to attend lectures and generally to inculcate themselves in the broader aspects of the military profession. Unlike officers of red-coated regiments, Rifles officers were expected to practice on the range, becoming marksmen like the men they commanded.

Having said all this, however they had originally gained their commission, it did not mean they considered themselves to be any less 'gentlemen' and socially distinct from the rank and file. In this respect the officers of the 95th were as rigidly traditional and conformist in their attitudes and behaviour as any in the British Army. Further, whether they had a supplementary income of their own or had to make their pay stretch, all officers were expected to maintain a certain standard of dress and lifestyle. Officers were obliged to purchase their own clothing and equipment, any newly appointed subaltern being expected to arrive at his company fully outfitted in a tailor-made uniform. Whilst the Rifle officer's uniform was free of the gold and silver metallic braid that adorned the uniforms of most commissioned ranks in the British Army, its intricate *hussar*-style decoration of black silk braid ensured it was both striking and costly.

Even on campaign, it was taken for granted that most officers would maintain at least one servant to ensure they were not troubled by such mundane matters as cooking, cleaning or erecting/dismantling their tent and other camping impedimenta. Rifleman Harris relates how one of his officers, Lieutenant Hill, had a black servant with him on the retreat to Corunna, 'a youth he had brought with him from Monte Video'. Further, whilst their men laboured with 60lbs of backpack, even the most junior subaltern had access to a mule to carry his belongings. Along with the mules, officers (even the most junior) had at least one horse, sometimes maintaining several, including one for the hunt. Finally, unlike their men, they were not restricted in the matter of wives, and numerous officers were accompanied to the Peninsula by their spouses, be this out of fidelity or a practical method of reducing expenditure.

The rigours of campaigning in the Peninsular ensured that even the most affluent and fashion-conscious gentleman ended up being barely identifiable as a soldier, let alone an officer, of the 95th. Lieutenant George Simmons wrote in one of his many letters a heartfelt description of his first experience of life on campaign, 'For the first time in my life I was treated with a bivouac. Hungry, wet, and cold, and without any covering, we lay down by the side of the river. I put one hand in my pocket and the other in my bosom, and lay shivering, and thinking of the glorious life of a soldier, until I fell fast asleep.'

Harris relates how, as Craufurd led the Light Brigade on its retreat to Vigo, 'The officers were also, for the most part, in a miserable plight. They were pallid, way-worn, their feet bleeding, and their faces overgrown with beards of many days' growth'. Wellington's later campaigns extracted no lesser price on martial appearance. Simmons provided one of the most vivid descriptions of his tattered outfit during the gruelling campaign against Massena 1810-11. 'My jacket is brown instead of green. Never was seen such a motley group of fellows...I am a perfect guerrilla, having broken my sword, lost my sash, and am as ragged as a sweep.' In fact, Simmons' locally-made outfit suffered further degradation when he burnt the bottom of his overalls whilst drying them over a camp-fire and he freely admitted that he was obliged to utilise captured French items, otherwise 'I should be nearly naked'.

Simmons was not alone in recording such telling reminiscences, although Kincaid's comments on his appearance whilst manning the Lines of Torres Vedras also reminds the reader he was a gentleman who relied upon others to maintain and clean his clothes. 'We had the utmost difficulty, however, in keeping up appearances in the way of dress. The jacket, in spite of shreds and patches, always maintained something of the original about it; but woe befell the regimental small-clothes, and they could only be replaced by very extraordinary apologies, of which I remember that I had two pair at this period, one of a common brown Portuguese cloth, and the other, or Sunday pair, of black velvet. We had no women with the regiment; and the ceremony of washing a shirt amounted to my servant taking it by the collar, and giving it a couple of shakes in the water, and then hanging it up to dry. Smoothing-irons were not the fashion of the times, and, if a fresh well-dressed aide-de-camp did occasionally come from England, we used to stare at him with about as much respect as Hotspur did at his "waiting gentlewoman".'

FIRING THE BAKER RIFLE

A priority for any soldier armed with a rifle is accuracy, and the emphasis on aimed fire went to

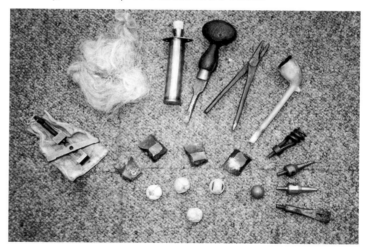

A selection of Baker rifle accessories: a brass oil bottle, tommy-bar, turnscrew, pincers, cleaning tow, worm, ball-pullers, wiping-eye, and a mainspring-clamp (the hole in the Baker rifle lock is traditionally filled with a nail to jam the mainspring for stripping and cleaning). The rifle-sized 'black floorstone' flints are circa 1806, recovered from a contemporary shipwreck and traced back to the Norfolk 'flint-knapper' who made them. The patched and lubricated balls are reproductions of actual patched rifle balls recently found 'in store' (the one in the centre is an original from the period and was mostly patched in pigskin, apparently smeared with a mixture of lard and tallow). What the original patches were stuck onto the bullets with defies laboratory identification – but it was later found to be very attractive to mice! *Richard Rutherford-Moore*

the very heart of his function. Thus it comes as no surprise that training highlighted the acquisition of such skills and Rifle units were issued a larger than usual allowance of ball and powder for target practice. When Surtees joined the Rifle Corps in June 1802, he relates how 'We immediately commenced our light drill, in which I took great delight; but most of all I liked the shooting at the target. As recruits, we were first drilled at what is termed the horse, ie a machine to assist young Riflemen in taking aim'. Surtees immediately impressed his officer with his marksmanship and was switched to a standard target.

At an initial distance of just 50 yards, Surtees fired 10 shots 'all of which hit the target, and two of which had struck the bull's eye'. Reflecting Stewart's stipulation that encouraging the soldier was the best way to improve performance, despite the short distance involved, the officer congratulated Surtees as a new recruit, 'unaccustomed to rifle-shooting' on his 'wonderful exhibition' and rewarded Surtees with a sixpence. Surtees recorded that he felt he deserved a larger reward! As it was, Surtees continued to improve his marksmanship, and along with his general attention to his duties, was soon rewarded with being appointed a 'Chosen Man'.

While there is no evidence they were worn on

Having loaded, taking careful aim was the whole *raison d'être* of the Rifleman. Here the recreated soldier has removed his shako to avoid the leather peak inhibiting his view, given the raised elevation of aim. *English Heritage*

campaign, Stewart certainly designated special distinctions that the finest shots could wear on their shako during training. To qualify for the lowest third class of marksman, the Rifleman had to place 'five shots out of six in the target two days out of three, firing from the shoulder at the distance of 100 yards'. To qualify for the second class and thus the right to wear a small white cockade, the Rifleman had to repeat this level of accuracy but at 150 yards. Finally, 'any Riflemen who puts four shots into the round target, or three in the body of the man in the canvas one, out of six...for two days practice out of three...will be ranked in the class of marksman, and wear the green cockade'.

That accuracy was paramount was reflected in the common practice, established with Frederick the Great's *Jäger* and subsequently emphasised by both Rottenberg and Stewart, that Riflemen were allowed to load their rifles however they wished. Unlike the infantry armed with smoothbore muskets, there was never a stipulated loading drill for Riflemen. Rather, provided their company officers were happy the individual Rifleman's method ensured an accurate shot, it was down to individual discretion. Unfortunately, despite the profusion of memoirs left by contemporary Riflemen, few specifically mention how they or others loaded their weapons, although at least seven variations have been identified from various sources.

Rifle-armed units were primarily meant to be marksmen, thus precise measurement of the powder charge was vital over any given distance. The powder horn carried from the cartridge belt was fitted with a brass funnel or 'charger' that 'threw' four and a half drams-- a hefty charge of powder. It would appear this corresponded to the service charge of issued cartridges and was quite capable of propelling a rifle bullet to the full distance of over 400 yards. Although Riflemen had initially been expected to load the ball, greased patch and powder

Opposite, like all black powder weapons, when the Baker was discharged the Rifleman was enveloped in a cloud of smoke. *English Heritage*

separately, by 1808 ball ammunition cartridges specifically made for the Baker rifle were available.

There is evidence that many Riflemen, particularly when first using them during training, found the service charge in these issued rounds excessive. The sharp kick that resulted did little for accuracy, particularly as the Rifleman would instinctively brace himself for the recoil. Many found that half the service charge, around two drams, was quite sufficient to attain a high level of accuracy up to 150 yards, yet avoid the sharp recoil. Thus it was apparently common for half the charge to be dumped onto the ground. As previously related, given that few Riflemen proved able to strike reliably a target much beyond 150 yards during training, the reduced charge made great sense in combat--the difficulty was gauging precisely just how much was loaded.

As the powder horn was issued with a charger that was not adjustable, it appears many Riflemen had small handmade 'chargers' suspended on a thong or string that permitted consistent charges of powder to be measured out from the powder horn or from issued rounds. The latter would still account for powder being discarded on the ground as once the ball was loaded, the partially-filled cartridge would still be thrown aside.

A further problem with the issued cartridges was that the enclosed lead ball was unpatched, the ball simply being wrapped in the paper of the cartridge itself. This did little for accuracy: the paper would often be stripped off the ball as it was rammed down thus allowing windage and fouling, or conversely, the paper would adhere to the ball as it left the bore, streaming behind it like a comet and ensuring it travelled in just about any direction except that in which it was aimed. Many Riflemen would ensure they had a ready supply of patches to wrap the ball to ensure the bore was cleaned of powder residue as it was rammed down and, when fired, the passage of the ball was lubricated with a minimum of windage.

Opposite, by the time of the Empire, specialised *voltigeurs*, distinguished by their yellow facings and epaulettes, were designated as skirmishers. As in the British Army, each battalion of French infantry included a company of such troops. By 1808 it was common practice to combine the *voltigeur* companies of a brigade or division so as to provide sufficient numbers simply to swamp the opposing skirmishers and clear the way for the assault.

Amongst the leading exponents of aimed fire was the author of *Scloppetaria*, Mark Beaufoy. The frontpiece of his book personified the skilled sharpshooter aspired to by many.

Next page, The preRevolutionary battalions of *chasseurs* ultimately became regiments of *Légér*. By the Empire, despite retaining their distinctive all blue uniform, the *Légér* were essentially line infantry. They are illustrated here engaged in furious combat with Prussian light infantry in 1807.

That the issued cartridge was still useful, despite part of its powder charge being routinely dumped and the ball being wrapped in paper, related to the size of the ball. Early on in the life of the Baker rifle, there had been some variation in the size of the ball, it often being slightly too large for the bore. This had required the issue of a wooden mallet to 'start' the ball home into the muzzle. Ezekiel Baker was contracted to supply small mallets at two and a half-pence each, although he admitted that 'they found them very inconvenient, and very soon dispensed with them'. Whilst steady manual pressure on the ramrod was meant to be sufficient, Costello included in his list of equipment in 1809 'a small wooden mallet to hammer the ball into the muzzle of our rifles'. However, other Riflemen did not include it in their otherwise specific lists of equipment and it would appear to have been an optional extra. Apart from the fact the issued rounds contained balls of a consistent size that did fit the bore, hammering a ball home would inevitably deform it, reducing its accuracy.

The experienced Rifleman, as reflected by William Green's account of the retreat to Vigo, carried a mix of '50 rounds of ball cartridge, 30 loose balls at our waist belt, and a flask [charger], and a horn of powder.' With a supply of pre-cut

Although only armed with smoothbore muskets (sergeants were issued rifled muskets as an apparent 'badge' of rank), this fact did not prevent French *voltigeurs* demonstrating their skill in utilising all available cover to bring directed fire to bear on enemy formations. Here a small body of *voltigeurs* is attempting to deliver what may be termed a 'harassing' fire on a battery of the Royal Horse Artillery.

greased patches in the butt box of the Baker, the veteran Rifleman could choose to load cartridges or their own measure of powder and patched ball: cartridges somewhat reduced the time it took to load, whilst loading the elements separately improved accuracy. The Rifleman was therefore able to adapt his method of loading to suit the needs of the moment, whether a higher rate of fire or careful marksmanship.

There was a fierce debate, both within and without the Rifle battalions, as to the advantages and disadvantages of the different methods and whether accuracy should always take priority over the rate of fire. Amongst the more interesting contributors to this debate were Ezekiel Baker, who wrote *Baker's Remarks on the Rifle*, and Mark Beaufoy, who wrote *Scloppetaria* under the *nom de plume* a 'Corporal of Riflemen'. The latter stated that accuracy should be the only deciding factor, not the rate of fire, an obvious priority when Riflemen were required to act as marksmen.

However, whilst some Baker rifles came with crude flip-up rear iron sights, most did not, given it was commonly held that sighting the rifle was superfluous when acting as skirmishers. It was found to be sufficient to aim at an opponent's shako at over 100 yards' range and where the belts crossed on the chest under 100 yards. It is possibly revealing that Surtees recorded that Major Wade and Rifleman Smeaton, two of the steadiest shots he knew, held targets for each other out to a maximum distance of 150 yards, but no further. Even Ezekiel Baker, when he conducted reliable tests, found '...200 yards the greatest range I could fire with certainty'.

Consequently, it was generally accepted that if a trained Rifleman could place a ball twice a minute somewhere in a man-sized target at ranges up to 150 yards, this was quite acceptable to enable them to have a comfortable edge over their French counterparts. Only first-class marksmen specifically directed by officers and supported by other Riflemen were given battlefield tasks of seeking selective targets such as officers, drummers, artillerymen and their gun-teams.

WHY NO FRENCH RIFLEMEN?

The debate in Britain over the best method of loading and targeting raises the question as to why the French did not arm a proportion of their otherwise highly capable light infantry with rifled weapons, choosing instead to rely on the standard smoothbore? In some respects the French Army had been ahead of the British in the evolution of light troops and there was a fulsome body of written doctrine from various military theorists that recognised and promoted the role of light troops. It is thus something of a surprise to find that, long before the French Revolution and Napoleon's rise to power, the French Army had rejected the rifle as an option even for its specialised *chasseurs*, and this despite seeing first-hand the impact of Riflemen in America.

The origins of this prejudice in the Army of the *Ancien Régime* dated back to the beginning of the 18th century when French military doctrine was already favouring deeper formations and the use of the *arme blanche* over weight of fire. Essentially two schools of thought had emerged by the 1700s: one that focused on linear formations drilled to deliver a constant hail of volley fire; the other on deeper and narrower formations that sought to break its opponents with the weight of its assault and the bayonet. As early as the battle of Blenheim in 1705, these contrasting tactical doctrines were obvious on the battlefields whenever British and French armies clashed. Although both doctrines underwent various modifications and developments, by the late 18th century the essential context was established.

Whilst this did not mean British officers were willing to bring a more open mind to the introduction of the rifle, it seems to have produced at least a few who were able to focus on its

advantages. Furthermore, the doctrines of linear formations and fire tactics had originated from the Dutch and German schools of military thought, and the British Army continued to look to these for new ideas. Thus once the Prussian, Hanoverian and other German forces began to introduce *Jäger*, it was only a matter of time before the British did so. Meanwhile the French continued to evolve largely around their own school of military doctrine, ensuring any debate was within the 'French' context. Thus Guilbert's *Tactique* produced the concept of the *l'ordre mixte*, a synthesis of column and line. Whilst a thick screen of light infantry was recognised as essential both to drive off opposing light infantry and generally to screen the deployment of the main body, it was not expected to have time effectively to engage as marksmen. Essentially, the formation of *l'ordre mixte* along with the general body of French military doctrine was premised on the assault, with light infantry expected to move and fire rapidly as the assault went in. What this context failed to do was produce any identifiable body of officers who argued for the adoption of the rifle, which was seen as pointless for the success of the rapid assault.

As Napoleon deployed ever more massive assault formations, shields of *voltigeurs* were drawn from entire brigades and divisions. At times entire regiments had to be deployed as skirmishers, whether they were a *légér* or standard *ligne* formation. Although Napoleon did write in December 1805 to his stepson Eugene that 'it is not enough that a soldier shoots, he must shoot well', apparently nothing was instituted to achieve such a goal. In comparison, Anglo-German linear and fire doctrines, whilst still quite capable of going over to the offensive, were essentially static and a screen of marksmen picking off opposing officers, drummers and the like was easily accommodated. It was in the Peninsula from 1808 that the two contrasting attitudes to the benefits of the rifle were tested on the battlefield.

RIFLEMAN
IN BATTLE

ARRIVING IN THE PENINSULA

Other than the Duke of York's participation in the
Lowlands from 1793-95, Britain in her war against
Napoleon had restricted her Army to limited
operations on the fringes of Europe until 1808.
Essentially, Britain had looked to her navy and
operations in the Caribbean as her main military
effort for much of the time. Political and financial
support for coalition after coalition of various
Continental powers was Britain's main contribution
to defeating the French in Europe, along with the
occasional landing of ground forces in what were
considered 'safe' operations. Whilst the Royal Navy,
particularly Nelson, brought victory after victory,
the operations undertaken by the Army were
hardly encouraging.

A British Army dispatched to South America
met with a crushing defeat at Buenos Aires in
July 1807. Another British Army successfully
collaborated with the Royal Navy at Copenhagen
the same year to prevent the Dutch fleet falling
under Napoleon's control. In both these operations,
companies of the 95th were in combat for the first
time. At Buenos Aires, as part of a 'Light Brigade'
under the command of Robert Craufurd (a fine
officer who was later to play a pivotal part in the
story of the 95th), the 95th found itself involved in
savage street fighting in which all were ultimately
captured. Meanwhile those detailed to support the
attack on Copenhagen were probably grateful to
have a far less eventful experience occupying the
place, serving in a brigade commanded by Major-
General Sir Arthur Wellesley (later the Duke of
Wellington). When they returned in late October,
they enjoyed a short respite before news arrived
of Napoleon's new adventure.

In December 1807 a French Army under General
Junot invaded Portugal. Once Britain was confident
the Portuguese Navy was safe, it initially did little
to respond to the country's call for assistance.
However, when Napoleon subsequently invaded
Spain and it, along with Portugal, rose in opposition,

the success of the Copenhagen operation was
sufficient to encourage the government to dispatch
forces to assist. One of the senior generals chosen
was an officer who had already distinguished
himself in both India and at Copenhagen the
previous year, the recently promoted Lieutenant-
General Sir Arthur Wellesley.

Although Rottenberg's battalion of the 60th
had been in service since 1797 and trained at
Shorncliffe, by 1808 it was still far from settled just
how any corps of Riflemen was to be deployed as
part of a British Army in the field. Essentially the
debate revolved around two issues: whether they
should be divided into small detachments to provide
expert marksmen throughout the Army or whether
they would serve as a unified regiment in a 'light
brigade'. These two schools of thought formed part
of an ongoing debate throughout the period. It is
certain that in 1808, as Wellesley waited in England
prior to being dispatched to the Peninsula, he is
recorded as stating that he considered the French
system of manoeuvre a 'false one as against
steady troops'. Once in theatre he quickly refined
his 'system' of deploying a staggered system of
infantry lines, supported by artillery, to defeat the
combination of French *voltigeurs* and column.
In this both light infantry and Rifleman played a key
role. Further, it became plain that Wellesley did not
come down on either side of the debate. Rather
both options were adopted as Wellesley organised
a light brigade, later a division, ultimately including
the entirety of the 95th, whilst the fifth battalion
60th and other rifle-armed units were divided
up and deployed as detached companies to
supplement the light infantry of each brigade.

Wellesley's men began disembarking in
Mondego Bay on 1 August. They included 936 men
of the fifth battalion of the 60th under Major William
Davy and four companies of the second battalion
95th Rifles, totalling 446 men under Major Robert
Travers. The grand total for the 60th was actually
well over 1,000 as they were accompanied ashore

by 60 wives and 50 children. Once ashore, the army was divided into brigades and interestingly both the 60th and 95th were placed with the 45th Foot (Nottinghamshire Regiment) as the Sixth or 'Light Brigade' Brigade under General Henry Fane. There seems to have been no suggestion the Rifleman should be apportioned out by company amongst the other brigades to give all a contingent. Rather, they were purposely massed together alongside a standard line regiment, albeit neither the 43rd or 52nd light infantry had yet arrived.

INTO ACTION

Having assembled some 13,000 British and 2,000 Portuguese troops (the latter under Colonel Sir Nicholas Trant), Wellesley, before he could commence his march on Lisbon, received the unwelcome news that three generals had been placed above him and he should expect their imminent arrival. Despite this slight, Wellesley chose to advance whilst awaiting his 'betters'.

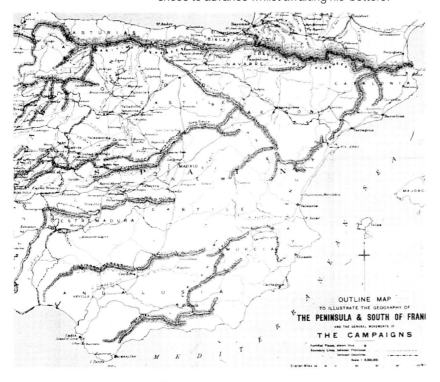

Above, the battlefields of Spain and Portugal were to see the British Rifleman come of age.

As Junot was still gathering his dispersed brigades, only General Delaborde's 5,000-strong division garrisoning Lisbon was available to move out to delay Wellesley. As Wellesley did not know of Delaborde's exact location, he promptly demonstrated that he considered Fane's Riflemen the designated advance-guard. On 15 August, having commenced his advance, eight companies from the 60th and 95th were dispatched to locate, engage and drive in the French outposts. Finding French piquets deployed at the windmill of Brilos just outside of the town of Obidos, the Riflemen pitched in, easily overwhelming the French and driving them back three miles. Harris recalled: 'Their skirmishers immediately commenced operations by raining a shower of balls upon us as we advanced, which we returned without delay.' During this sharp exchange Lieutenant Ralph Bunbury of the 95th had the dubious distinction of being the very first British officer killed in the Peninsula when he was shot through the head.

The pursuit was decidedly over keen. Lieutenant John Cox was honest when he wrote in his journal '...a rapid advance of the Riflemen drew the French from all points of their posts, but being rather too elevated with this, our first collision with the foe, we dashed along the plain after them like young soldiers.' When the Riflemen came upon the battalion and supporting cavalry that formed Delaborde's rearguard, they found themselves in a severe fire-fight that they were in danger of losing, with cavalry hovering on their flanks ready to pounce. Harris continued his account: 'I had never heard such a tremendous noise as the firing made on this occasion, and I occasionally observed that the men on both sides of me were falling fast.' The Riflemen were only able safely to disengage themselves when General Sir Brent Spencer brought up a brigade to rescue them.

In their first engagement in the Peninsula, the Riflemen's total losses were 23 from the 60th and six from the 95th. Wellesley, whilst admiring the spirit of the ordinary Rifleman, was not impressed with the judgement of their officers, as revealed in his report to the government. 'The affair of the advanced posts of yesterday evening was unpleasant, because it was quite useless; and was occasioned, contrary to orders, solely by the imprudence of the Officers, and the dash and eagerness of the men: they behaved remarkably well and did some execution with their rifles.' Equally, he wrote to the Duke of Richmond that it had been 'foolishly brought on by the over-eagerness of the Riflemen' albeit they behaved 'remarkably well, but not with great prudence.' As the war progressed, the 95th were often to act thus, their exuberance and view of themselves as an élite ensuring they continually pushed themselves to the fore in just about every engagement, resulting in heavy casualties from the musketry their rifles were designed to out-range.

As Delaborde was subsequently discovered to have fallen back three miles to Roliça, 17 August provided both the 95th and 60th a second opportunity to test their skills against their French counterparts. Delaborde's main position was a ridge rising above a sandy plain across which Wellesley would advance. Roughly a mile in front of the ridge lay an isolated eminence on whose side-slope lay Roliça, which had a fine view across the sandy plain. The road traversing the plain continued to the ridge which it crossed in a shallow gorge, on either side of which were villages, Columbeira to the right and Zambugeira to the left. Given Delaborde knew his division was outnumbered three to one, he decided upon a staggered defence, starting with the eminence upon which Roliça stood, from which he would fall back to the ridge. The ridgeline was only three-quarters of a mile in length and boasted a fairly precipitous slope dotted with thickets and brushwood, thus making a strong defensive position. Delaborde's decision to defend this ridge was partly taken in the hope that a second French division of 5,000 men under

General Loison would arrive and he could inflict a sharp rebuff to the British; in this he was to be disappointed as Loison was too far away to make the union in time.

Delaborde knew his advance position at Roliça was little more than a delaying tactic, given Wellesley could easily outflank it on both sides, which is indeed what he did, drawing up his army in a crescent formation with the centre refused whilst the wings moved to either side of Roliça. Wellesley placed Fane's Rifleman on the centre left in an extended skirmish line, the 60th on the right, the 95th on the left, to assault Roliça. Captain Jonathan Leach left a vivid account of this advance: 'We had to ascend first one mountain so covered with brushwood that our legs were ready to sink under us, the enemy on the top of it lying down in the heath keeping up a hot and constant fire in our face and the men dropping all round us.' But even as the Riflemen commenced exchanging shots with the *voltigeurs*, Delaborde ordered his men to retire to their main position on the ridge, easily avoiding Wellesley's carefully constructed envelopment. Realising the strength of Delaborde's defences on the wooded heights above Columbeira, Wellesley was obliged to spend half the morning re-arranging

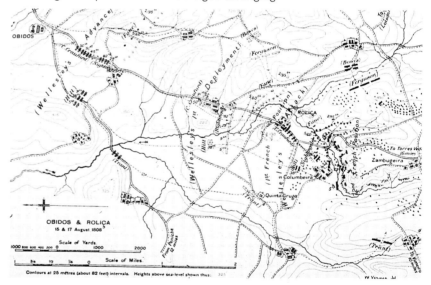

The rolling series of actions from Brilos through to Roliça marked the debut of both the 60th and 95th in the Peninsula.

his men to attempt to take it. Wishing to avoid heavy casualties, Wellesley intended that Trant's Portuguese and General Ferguson with two British brigades and three companies of the 60th would march across the hills to the right and left respectively to outflank Delaborde and oblige him to retire. The remainder of his forces were to wait on either side of the road until the turning movement was achieved, at which point they would attack and hopefully fall upon the French as they attempted to fall back. Fane's Riflemen were drawn up to the left of the road to await this moment.

Matters did not quite work out like this as both turning movements were delayed. There were four

gullies or ravines leading up the ridge from the British position and British troops moved up each whilst Delaborde's four defending battalions were forced to retire. The 60th and 95th assaulted the gully on the far left, providing the Riflemen with an excellent opportunity to put into practice all they had been taught. Whilst the 9th and 29th Foot in the gullies on the right made a series of brave but bloody frontal assaults (the 29th suffered 190 casualties), on the left the 60th and 95th deployed into extended order and fought their way to the top. Cox wrote that they were '...sharply engaged throughout with large bodies of *Voltigeurs* who were strongly posted in the steep hills, vineyards and enclosures from which they were successively driven.' After two hours of intense combat, British troops finally managed to make lodgements on the ridge, and with Ferguson belatedly turning Delaborde's left, he was obliged to retreat.

Harris left a vivid account of the whole action from Roliça to the ridge that makes it clear the British Riflemen were exchanging fire with the French *voltigeurs* well within smoothbore range, that is 50-60 yards. 'Soon afterwards the firing commenced, and we had advanced pretty close upon the enemy. Taking advantage of whatever cover I could find, I threw myself down behind a small bank, where I lay so secure, that, although the Frenchmen's bullets fell pretty thickly around, I was enabled to knock several over without being dislodged; in fact, I fired away every round I had in my pouch whilst lying on this spot.' From this it is obvious Harris not only loaded and fired his weapon whilst prone, but that he occupied this single vantage point for at least one hour (given even an optimistic rate of fire). He continued, 'At length, after a sharp contest, we forced them to give ground, and, following them up, drove them from their position in the heights, and hung upon their skirts till they made another stand, and then the game began again.' That the range was well within that of a standard smoothbore was attested

Top, a view of Delaborde's second position at Roliça, 17 August 1808, looking across the French left flank. Wellesley's troops attacked from right to left, flushing the French from the top of these heights. The village of Columbeira is just visible to the right. *Ian Fletcher Battlefield Tours*

Bottom, Roliça, looking along the second French position from their left. Four companies of the 2/95th attacked the far end of these heights. *Ian Fletcher Battlefield Tours*

to by the death alongside Harris of Rifleman Joseph Cochan who, whilst swallowing a draught from his canteen, 'a bullet went through the canteen, and perforating his brain, killed him in a moment.' Leach told a very similar story, although it was a fellow officer offering Leach the drink of wine and this good Samaritan was fortunate to only be shot through the hand. In fact both 60th and 95th suffered a significant number of casualties from the *voltigeurs'* musketry, losing 66 and 50 men respectively, or nearly 10% of the number engaged. Thus, whilst it was obvious the 95th were fully utilising the accuracy of their Baker rifles, their potentially greater range was immaterial, hence the use of a reduced charge, suggested earlier, was logical.

Before leaving the action at Roliça, it is worth relating Harris's account of the conclusion to the day that proved the 95th could use their bayonets just as effectively as their red coated comrades. Finding the *voltigeurs* fighting determinedly from behind a small rise above the village of Zambugeira, the Riflemen's blood was up. 'So angry did they become...One skirmisher jumped up and rushed forward crying "Over boys! Over, Over!" Instantly the whole line responded...They ran along the grass like wildfire and dashed at the rise, fixing their sword-bayonets as they did so. The French light bobs, unable to stand the sight, turned about and fled.' The Riflemen had little time to celebrate. Just a few days later a much larger action was to be fought at Vimeiro where Junot had assembled his whole force and again the 60th and 95th were in the thick of it.

VIMEIRO

Although Wellesley had finally been superseded by Lieutenant-General Sir Harry Burrard's arrival on 20 August (along with reinforcements), this gentleman chose to remain that night on his ship in the bay overlooked by Vimeiro, leaving Wellesley to command till the next day. This apparently simple

decision had a tremendous impact upon destiny (there are few that have ever heard of General Burrard!). During the 20th Wellesley chose to re-organise rifle deployment by attaching one company of the 60th to each of the other seven brigades respectively, leaving just three companies of the 60th with Fane. There is no doubt Wellesley had recognised the value of his Riflemen and at long last the original idea of giving every skirmish line a contingent of marksmen was a reality and this remained so throughout the rest of the war.

The next day was to see the battle of Vimeiro and this time it was the French who were to do the attacking, Wellesley deploying the sort of defensive tactics that were to become so familiar in the years to come. The hill Wellesley chose as the centre of his position lay just in front of the village of Vimeiro, which sat on a well-marked line of heights. This hill was dotted with vineyards and thickets amongst open fields. To defend this, Wellesley positioned six guns, three 6lbs and three 9lbs, along with seven battalions of Anstruther and Fane's brigades: the former included the recently arrived second battalions of the 43rd and 52nd Light Infantry whilst the latter deployed three companies of the 60th, one company of the first battalion 95th and four of the second battalion. Thus on one hill stood much of the British Army's specialist light infantry

At Vimeiro, this is the view that Fane's Riflemen would have had as the French advanced towards them. The village of Vimeiro lies behind the camera. *Ian Fletcher Battlefield Tours*

and Riflemen who were presented with a classic terrain to defend. It was against this hill that Junot chose to launch his main assault by Loison and Delaborde's divisions.

Fane deployed most of the 60th and 95th as a very thick skirmish line at the foot of the hill and a piquet line deployed forward of this, with only a few companies held as a reserve at the top of the slope with the 50th Foot. Four French battalions approached in the standard formation of battalion columns, each heavily screened by *voltigeurs*. The commander of Harris's company, Captain Jonathan Leach, gave a vivid account of this: '...about seven in the morning the enemy began to appear on some hills in our front, and shortly... several immense columns made their appearance towards the right and centre... The pickets being only a handful of men by way of a look-out to prevent surprise, were ordered to check the French columns by a running fire as much as possible, and to retreat firing.' So rapid was the French advance that a number

of Riflemen were made prisoners, the first captured in the Peninsula.

Fane's section of the hill was now assaulted by two of these columns under the command of General Thomières. Despite the strength of their skirmish line, the Riflemen were forced to retire by the *voltigeurs*, who were closely supported by solid columns of troops. As Leach related: 'We remained in the wood until several men were killed and the shots flew like hail, when the Field Officer of the pickets ordered us to retreat precipitately as our Artillery dared not fire a shot at the French columns (which were pressing hastily on) till we fell back. We retreated down a vineyard and up another hill before we could gain the British lines, the whole time exposed to the fire of a battalion of infantry...'.

The account left by Harris suggests the Riflemen made several stands as they retired and that the rate of fire was not unimportant. 'I myself was soon so hotly engaged, loading and firing away, enveloped in the smoke I created, and the cloud which hung about me from the continued fire of my comrades, that I could see nothing for a few minutes but the red flash of my own piece amongst the white vapour clinging to my very clothes.' As at Roliça, Harris chose, where possible, to fight prone. 'The French, in great numbers, came steadily down upon us, and we pelted away upon them like a shower of leaden hail. Under any cover we could find we lay; firing one moment, jumping up and running for it the next.' Harris suggests the Riflemen again chose not to utilise the full range of the Baker: '...we halted and made another stand for when once engaged, we never went further from the enemy than we could possibly help.' According to a captured captain of *voltigeurs* who was under this fire, the recipients certainly did not feel they could adequately respond, suggesting the accuracy of the Baker was decisively superior. The captain had been '...sent out to skirmish against some of these in green. Grasshoppers I call them; you call them Riflemen. They were behind every bush and

The battle of Vimeiro saw the 60th and 95th severely engaged in both defensive and aggressive actions.

stone and soon made sad havoc among my men, killing all the officers of my company, and wounding myself without [us] being able to do them any injury. This drove me to distraction.'

Despite the *voltigeur* captain's comments, Thomières' men swept forward. As Leach related: 'Some heavy masses of infantry, preceded by a swarm of light troops, were advancing with great resolution, and with loud cries of "Vive l'Empereur! En avant" etc. against the hill on which our brigade was posted. In spite of the deadly fire which several hundred Riflemen kept upon them, they continued to press forward with great determination.' As Thomières' columns finally approached the top of the slope, both the *voltigeurs* and Riflemen cleared away to the flanks. At this point Fane launched the 50th Foot and reserve companies of Riflemen at the head of each column, both of which collapsed and fled down the hill in utter disorder.

This was far from the end of it, as Junot ordered forward a second assault. A still common practice in the French Army was to mass together each battalions' élite companies into composite battalions (a practice long since abandoned by the British). Two such battalions of grenadiers now marched forward in battalion column against the hill under Colonel St Clair. They were promptly shot to pieces by the converging fire of the 52nd, 97th, 60th and 95th as well as having the dubious honour of being the first to feel the effect of the newly developed shrapnel shell discharged from the British guns. St Clair's grenadiers barely reached half way up the slope before breaking to the rear.

In a last desperate attempt to win, Junot launched his remaining two battalions of grenadiers under Colonel Maransin into a gap on the left of Fane's position in an attempted outflanking movement, trusting that in battalion column they would move more rapidly than any British defensive move. This assault was led in person by the commander of the reserve, General

Kellermann, and whilst it was initially free of opposition, the grenadiers soon came under intensive flanking fire as British light infantry and Riflemen displayed their ability at rapid re-deployment. Anstruther had the 43rd double over into the cemetery of Vimeiro from where it poured fire into the left of the leading grenadier battalion. Meanwhile, further to Wellesley's left stood General Acland's brigade (recently arrived from Britain) which included two companies of the first battalion 95th. Acland dispatched both, along with the light companies of the 2nd and 20th Foot, whom he directed onto the grenadiers' right flank. He supported these with two guns. Although taking heavy casualties from the flanking fire, the grenadiers reached the eastern end of Vimeiro itself before their columns lost cohesion. However, they did not flee and there now followed an intense and confusing combat amongst the houses and walls of the village. Here, as at Roliça, the Riflemen demonstrated the need for the Baker's bayonet as they and the light infantry fought at close quarters with their opponents. In the end, Kellermann's grenadiers gave up the struggle and retired, still under orders, back to their start line.

Whilst there was still much hard fighting elsewhere on the battlefield, the 60th and 95th were done for the day. As during their two previous actions in the preceding week, they had been used as light infantry battalions rather than deployed as marksmen along the generality of the line to supplement red-coated skirmishers. This was probably inevitable, given they were embodied as coherent battalions, each with a single hierarchy and were so treated by the commanding general. However it did mean the potential range of the Baker rifle was hardly utilised, thus begging the question of whether the additional expense of specialist Rifle battalions was worth it if utilised in this way. As at Roliça, both the 60th and 95th suffered significant casualties from their smoothbore-armed French opponents.

Just how serious is attested to by the fact that all the 95th's losses were from the four companies of the second battalion losing fully a third of those engaged with 37 dead and 43 wounded. This also raised the question as to whether the Baker was even managing to inflict more casualties due to its greater accuracy, given much of the fighting was at ranges where the greater number of smoothbores being discharged potentially made up for its   . inaccuracy. An analysis of the cost effectiveness of the rifle versus the smoothbore would have been an interesting exercise, given the increased financial cost of the former, in addition to the training the Rifleman required to use it effectively!

CRAUFURD AND THE LIGHT BRIGADE

Changes now occurred that were to have a fundamental impact on the future utilisation of the Rifle battalions. Due to the dispute over the Convention of Cintra (Wellesley's seniors, in their wisdom, agreed to evacuate Junot's defeated army and its plunder back to France on Royal Navy ships), Wellesley briefly departed the scene to return to Britain. This left the recently arrived Sir John Moore to take command on 6 October and, as further troops and generals had arrived from Britain, he undertook a major re-organisation of British forces. Whilst it appears the 60th were due to constitute part of Moore's forces, due to the unspecified 'misbehaviour' and 'irregularities' of five of its companies, on 5 December the whole battalion was ordered back to Lisbon as escort to a convoy. Having joined some 8,000 other British troops under General Sir John Cradock billeted in and around Lisbon, they remained there well into 1809. During this sojourn, under the able command of Major Davy, the 60th discharged a number of miscreants and re-built its battered ranks. It should be added that Davy was careful to maintain its German character, writing to Colonel Bathurst requesting that 'I might have it in my power to select men fit for the service, and therefore request he will

mention that the Austrian-Hungarians, together with all Germans north of the Rhine, particularly Hessians, are those upon which we can place the most dependence.'

Even without the 60th, Moore was the first British general to have no shortage of either Riflemen or light infantry, with the first and second battalions 95th, the 1st and 2nd Light Battalions of the KGL, and both battalions of the 43rd and 52nd. Yet he still chose to organise all his light troops, including the Riflemen, as specialist formations rather than distribute them as marksmen to every brigade. Thus two 'Flank Brigades' were created, the first under the recently arrived Colonel Robert Craufurd, composed of the first battalion 43rd, second battalion 52nd and second battalion 95th, the latter numbering 750 men in its eight companies The second was composed of the two Light Battalions of the KGL under Brigadier-General Sir Charles Alten (a Hanoverian officer). Over the next few years both these officers were to establish reputations as experts in the war of outposts and reconnaissance. Furthermore, the soldiers of the KGL were to continue the long-standing dynamic by which German military professionalism continued to prove it still had important lessons to teach its British cousins.

Robert Craufurd was already recognised as a leading officer of light troops and had an opportunity to lead the 95th in action the previous year at Buenos Aires. It had not been the British Army's finest day and Craufurd had been fortunate not to see that debacle end his career. Upon his return from captivity, utilising his circle of influential family connections, he secured appointment to the staff of his friend Sir John Moore in Spain. Arriving with Sir David Baird's 15,000-strong reinforcements in October 1808, amongst which were 11 companies of the 95th, he tapped his friendship with Moore to secure his appointment as Brigadier-General and commander of the newly created Light Brigade. It should be added that the

Robert Craufurd proved an inspirational if unrelenting commander of possibly the finest force of light troops ever fielded.

95th had also been joined by its Lieutenant-Colonel, Thomas Sidney Beckwith, who was to play an important part alongside Craufurd in shaping the role of the Riflemen in the field. An extremely popular and able officer, Beckwith had transferred into the original Experimental Rifle Corps from the 71st Foot in August 1800 as a brevet Major. Having become Lieutenant-Colonel of the newly titled 95th Rifles in January 1803, he was already admired for his qualities of leadership, unfailing bravery, yet sincere humanity. Under Beckwith, the 95th continued to abhor corporal punishment and stress marksmanship.

Whilst Craufurd's Light Brigade fought no pitched battles during Moore's abortive campaign in Spain, the bitter retreat gave them ample opportunity to demonstrate their skills as a rearguard. Craufurd and Alten's light brigades, operating alongside the five light cavalry regiments under Lord Henry William Paget (later the Earl of Uxbridge), displayed great skill in all aspects of the operation of light troops, generally besting their veteran French opponents at every turn. At the culmination of Moore's abortive march to link up with Joachim Blake's Spanish Army (they had been decimated by the French) at Sahagun on 21 December, Paget's 10th and 15th Hussars routed a strong force of French Dragoons.

Throughout the retreat Craufurd maintained the closest grip possible on the men under his command, personally supervising every detail.

Moore subsequently withdrew his 30,000-strong army to avoid encirclement by the 150,000 French troops Napoleon was directing against him. Paget scored another stunning victory at Benavente on 29 December when the 10th Hussars and 3rd Dragoons of the KGL defeated Napoleon's own *Chasseurs-à-Cheval* of the Guard and captured their commander, General Lefebvre-Desnouëttes. In both these actions detachments of the 95th provided infantry support.

As 1809 dawned, Craufurd and Alten's light brigades were ordered to take the road to Vigo, the duty of providing the rearguard now falling to Major-General Sir Edward Paget's reserve division (brother of William Paget), which included the first battalion of the 95th under Lieutenant-Colonel Beckwith. Craufurd's renown as a martinet came to the fore during this period, the 95th being on the receiving end of his violent temper just as often as other units. Even the 95th's officers had to be careful, there being an oft-repeated story of an unwell officer who, already suffering in the cold and rain, walked around a small stream whilst his men marched through it. Spotted by Craufurd, who had issued strict orders that no-one, including officers, could break ranks, the luckless subaltern was forced to march back and forth through the stream several times before Craufurd grimly permitted him to proceed. This strict code of discipline earned Craufurd his famous nickname 'Black Bob' that remained with him until his death. Craufurd's harsh discipline, however, helped ensure that of the 2,262 soldiers he began the campaign with in October, having been evacuated from Vigo, Craufurd's Light Brigade returned to England having lost only 342 men.

AMAZING SHOT

It was a few days after the separation from Craufurd and Alten that one of Beckwith's Riflemen performed one of the war's most famous displays of marksmanship, robbing the French light cavalry of one of its most able generals. After the capture of Lefebvre-Desnouëttes, command of the French advance guard fell to General Auguste de Colbert, who was soon pressing Paget's men hard. On 3 January some six miles east of Villafranca, where the road crossed the river Cua over a narrow bridge at the village of Cacabelos, Paget decided to inflict a sharp rebuff to the French pursuit by laying an ambush. Paget placed a six-gun horse artillery battery on a low ridge overlooking the bridge with the 28th Foot positioned to block the road itself just below. On either side of the road, deployed amongst the hedges and vineyard walls, were the first battalion of the 52nd and much of the 95th. Meanwhile, still covering the retreat of the last few stragglers were two companies of the 95th and a squadron of the 15th Hussars on the other side of the river. At around 3pm Colbert arrived at the head of two regiments of *chasseurs à cheval* and some companies of *voltigeurs*. Colbert immediately charged the single squadron of the 15th Hussars who were easily broken and forced to flee across the river. The two supporting companies of the 95th attempted to make a stand in the main street of Cacabelos and managed to shoot down a few of the *chasseurs*, but being heavily outnumbered, they were almost immediately ridden down and cut to pieces, losing fully a third of their number killed or captured.

Possibly emboldened by this easy victory, Colbert, despite knowing significant infantry and artillery re-enforcements under General Merle were approaching, chose to carry the bridge and British positions across the river with the troops he had. In gallant style he led his men in a charge over the bridge, the troopers formed up just four abreast, up the road and straight into a deadly crossfire. The head of the column was cut down by artillery fire, the rest managing to cross and hurl themselves up the road. Now the 52nd and 95th poured in well-directed fire from either flank, emptying many saddles and bringing the French advance to a halt.

At this point Colbert was riding up and down, desperately trying to urge his men on and thus he became a very specific Rifleman's target.

Thomas Plunket was already a well-known character in the 95th. Like so many others, he was an Irishman recruited from the militia and Costello recalls: 'I had, more than once, heard of a man of the name of Tom Plunket, and had heard him eulogised by the men for his courage. He was a smart, well-made fellow, about middle height and in the prime of manhood; with a clear grey eye and handsome countenance. He was a general favourite with both officers and men, besides being the best shot in the regiment'. Plunket's reputation as an excellent shot was now to be fully vindicated. As the French cavalry milled about on the road, Plunket crawled across the snow-covered ground until he had a clear shot of Colbert. Then, lying on his back with the sling of his rifle wrapped round his foot, he took careful aim and shot Colbert dead in his saddle from well over 300 yards, the ball smashing into Colbert's head just above the left eye. As Colbert's body fell to the ground his orderly trumpeter dashed over to ascertain his commander's state. Plunket, having re-loaded, shot him through the head also before dashing back to the security of a nearby wall from where he and the others continued to shoot down French troopers until the

Tom Plunket's feat of marksmanship in shooting Colbert at Cacabelos was but the most famous of his many such kills. This method of steadying his aim was one of several taught to all Riflemen. *Peter Newark's Military Pictures*

Next page, James Beadle's famous painting of *The Rearguard*, showing the 95th during the retreat to Corunna, conveys the bitter winter weather they had to cope with. *Royal Green Jackets Museum*

survivors fell back over the bridge, leaving over 200 men dead and wounded on the field.

Whether true or not, Costello (who was not present) told a somewhat picturesque version of this event. Costello first commented that Colbert, although 'frequently aimed at by our men, ...seemed to bear a charmed life, and invariably escaped'. Next, 'Paget rode up to the rifles and offered his purse to any man who would shoot him.' Having dispatched Colbert and returned to the ranks, 'Our General immediately gave Tom the purse he had promised, with encomiums upon his gallantry'. In fact, Plunket already had a reputation for shooting enemy officers in doubtful circumstances. At Buenos Aires in July 1807, having taken position on the roof of the Convent of Santa Domingo, he shot down every single Spaniard he saw, at least 20 he later claimed. At one point this included an officer who appeared under a flag of truce to request the British surrender, Plunket's only comment being 'I'll have a slap at the fellow with the white handkerchief', which he did, mortally wounding him. Whatever the truth, at Cacabelos (a British aristocrat and general paying a common Rifleman to assassinate a fellow aristocrat and officer seems highly implausible), Plunket was rewarded with a set of corporal stripes and seemed destined for higher things. But, like so many other soldiers, drink was his great weakness and before long he was just a Rifleman once more, although he continued to claim a heavy toll of enemy officers right through the Peninsula War. His vices ultimately caused his discharge in 1817 when he was described as 'being a very bad character and being nearly worn out in the service'. Plunket was one of only a handful of Riflemen in the 95th renowned for marksmanship over extended distances, that is, in excess of 200 yards. It is partially for this fact he was so well known.

Whatever the truth of Colbert's death, his demise blunted the French assault. While Moore withdrew his troops, the 95th conducted a sharp duel with the *4eme Légér*, the latter losing some 60 *chasseurs*

to well-directed fire. The overall action cost the 95th dear, two officers being wounded (one mortally), two sergeants and 17 Rifleman killed outright, whilst foue sergeants and 44 Rifleman were captured, most being wounded. Yet the sharp rebuff given the French at Cacabellos and the continued sterling service of Paget's men ensured the only subsequent losses on the retreat to their pursuers were exhausted and drunken stragglers.

CORUNNA

At the battle of Corunna, the 95th, along with the 52nd, were to fight an action that could almost have been designed as a model field exercise at Shorncliffe. Initially, Beckwith's battalion formed part of the reserve under Paget, but as the battle opened, Beckwith was ordered to advance forward on the far right of Moore's line, up the shallow valley cut by the Monelos Stream. This he did by deploying the entire battalion of some 750 Riflemen in skirmish order across the valley, a width of around half-a-mile, thus requiring a minimum spacing between files of two to three yards. The Riflemen's first contact was an almost unique contest between a dismounted regiment of French dragoons, whose muskets proved no match for the Baker. The dragoons retired to Beckwith's right where, despite remaining a threat, the 95th continued its advance in skirmish order, now supported by the 52nd deployed to their rear.

Having next reached the walls enclosing the village of Someso, both the 52nd and 95th came upon the now exposed left flank of the *47eme Ligne* who were advancing in column to assault Moore's main position. Bringing the *47eme* under a sharp fire, they caused its assault to stall and it retired. Now sweeping past the village of Someso, two further French dragoon regiments attempted to assault Beckwith's front, but the broken nature of the ground severely impeded their mounts whilst it allowed the Riflemen to shoot down numerous troopers. Having driven off two attempted assaults

The Church of Santa Domingo, Buenos Aires, taken in 1942. This is the church where Craufurd and many of the 95th Rifles were trapped and forced to surrender during Whitelock's failed attack on the city in July 1807. It is possible to still see bullet holes on the left-hand tower.
Ian Fletcher Battlefield Tours

Opposite, despite the unrelenting pace of the retreat to Corunna reducing their clothes to rags, the 95th continued to harass the pursuing French all the way to the coast. However, Harris, amongst many commentators, relates how many were obliged to wrap strips of cloth around their boots to hold them together, some even being reduced to hobbling through the snow in bare feet.

by the dragoons, the 52nd and 95th continued forward until they became engaged with two composite battalions of French *voltigeurs*. After a protracted fire-fight, the *voltigeurs* gave way, and now, supported by further regiments from Paget's reserve, the 52nd and 95th, still deployed as skirmishers, drove far onto the French left where they remained engaged until nightfall and the battle's end.

This remarkable action cost relatively few casualties, despite Beckwith having advanced over one and a half miles in almost continuous action. The 95th's casualties were just 12 killed and 33 wounded, whilst their close companions for much of the action, the 52nd, also with a strength of some 750 men, reported just five killed and 33 wounded. Across the whole battlefield the French Army had been decisively repulsed, but the death of Moore, their mentor at Shorncliffe, was keenly felt by the soldiers of the two regiments. While no further casualties were suffered prior to their evacuation on the 12th, the campaign cost one further key player in the establishment of the 95th itself, none other than Coote Manningham. Promoted major-general in 1805, he had commanded a brigade in Moore's army throughout the campaign. Although only forty-two years old, his earlier service in the Caribbean had left his health permanently weakened by wounds and illness. Although he survived the retreat to embark with the rest of the army at Corunna, the stress and exertions of the campaign proved too much for his enfeebled constitution. After eight months of chronic illness, he finally died at his home in Maidstone on 26 August 1809.

WELLESLEY'S RETURN

Although Wellesley had, prior to 1808, expressed his opinion that the French tactical system was false and could be defeated, his experiences of 1808 refined his thoughts. Equally, from their first arrival in the Peninsula in 1808, the Riflemen's skills as marksmen had been emphasised and Wellesley built this into what proved to be a winning system on the battlefield against French columns screened by *voltigeurs*. From Wellesley's return in 1809, detached companies of Riflemen covered the front of Wellesley's line, exacting a heavy toll on any attacking French formation. Meanwhile, the 95th again formed part of a brigade of light infantry tasked to perform a multitude of roles both on and off the battlefield. In particular, it provided Wellesley with a sufficiently large mass of light troops able, if required, to swamp and suppress opposing bodies of French light troops.

On 4 May, shortly after his arrival, one of Wellesley's first general orders was to re-institute the deployment he had chosen the previous year after disembarkation at Mondego Bay by distributing the 60th by company to each brigade of the army. Whilst Major Davy continued 'to superintend the economy and discipline of the whole battalion...' and retained five companies as part of Major-General Tilson's brigade, the balance of five companies were placed under the field command of each respective brigade commander. Henceforth, each was deployed to support the light companies of their respective brigade to provide a uniform sprinkling of marksmen. This practice remained a standard feature of Wellesley's Army

Above, the transports that were to evacuate Moore's men had to wait in the harbour whilst the battle raged in the hills above.

Right, Lieutenant-Colonel Sir William Davy commanded the fifth battalion of the 60th when it first landed in the Peninsula. **Royal Green Jackets Museum**

until the very end in April 1814. As early as the successful crossing of the Douro and capture of Oporto on 12 May, Major-General Hill had occasion to congratulate by name Captain Wend's company of the 60th that had fought so furiously when clearing the streets of Soult's men.

The men of the 95th had only a brief respite in England, for having landed in early February, they had only until late May before the first battalion, along with the first battalions of the 43rd and 52nd, were ordered back to Portugal under Craufurd's command. Landing at Lisbon on 2 July 1809, the Light Brigade, described by Leach as 'the finest and most splendid brigade that ever took the field', undertook a gruelling march of 42 miles under 26 hours in the July heat in a desperate attempt to join Wellesley at Talavera. Although at times averaging 30 miles per day, Wellesley fought and won the battle while the Light Brigade was still pouring sweat on the road. The Rifleman of the 60th performed sterling service in their absence, being amongst the few regiments mentioned by name in Wellesley's official dispatch to the British government.

It was during the gruelling march to Talavera, that Craufurd issued his *Standing Orders*, a set of notes that were now to govern all matters relating to marches, camp layout, the conduct of outpost duty and even official documentation. Prefaced on Moore's own instructions for light infantry, despite an initially hostile reception, they became the bedrock document of the Light Brigade and later the Light Division, remaining in circulation decades later. Further, in respect of the 95th, Craufurd

J.P. Beadle sketched this view of the battlefield of Corunna in 1912 from the plateau north of the village of Elviña. By dusk Beckwith's Riflemen occupied a position to the right of centre in the hills in the distance.

stressed the primacy of aimed fire, going as far as prohibiting the use of 'tap loading', that is striking the butt of the rifle on the ground to cause the ball to be shaken down the barrel rather than using the ramrod. Whilst this method certainly saved time loading, as the ball usually ended up only part of the way down the barrel, it made accurate shooting an impossibility.

BARBA DEL PUERCO

Despite his victory at Talavera, the vagaries of Spanish support forced Wellesley to fall back to take up a defensive posture on the Portuguese border. Wellesley, who now became Viscount Wellington of Talavera, promoted Craufurd to command of the Third Division (its previous commander, Major-General Mackenzie, having been killed at Talavera). With the subsequent addition of Hew Ross's troop of Royal Horse Artillery, the 1st Hussars of the KGL and British-trained third battalion of Portuguese *Chasseurs*, this became the Light Division. The latter had been raised in November 1808 as one of six light infantry battalions, all trained and partially officered by the British Army. Re-titled *Caçadores* ('hunters' in Portuguese) in 1809, they were armed and equipped as Rifleman, albeit in brown uniforms (a colour of cloth plentiful in Portugal). They were to

earn the admiration and trust of their counterparts in the 60th and 95th and a further six battalions were raised in 1811 (although due to a shortage of Baker rifles, a proportion appear to have had to make do with standard Brown Bess muskets). For now, whilst the main British Army was stationed in the Upper Mondego valley, Craufurd's new command took up advanced positions between the rivers Agueda and Coa during December.

The months of January, February and March 1810 put all Craufurd's soldiers, but especially the 95th, to their sternest test yet in proving their worth as light troops. With a frontage of some 40 miles, Craufurd's men had both to scout French positions for information whilst preventing their opponents penetrating British lines on a similar mission. As the country was open yet rolling and broken in make-up, Craufurd chose to hold most of his infantry back, relying on a thin screen of cavalry at his front. With beacons prepared on suitable heights to communicate rapidly the approach of an enemy, the Light Division could be under arms and ready to march in seven minutes. The only infantry placed forward in direct contact with the French were four companies of the 95th covering the bridge at Barba del Puerco. This detachment was fated to fight one of the classic outpost actions of the war.

The village of Barba del Puerco stands near the junction of the Agueda and Douro rivers and a critical bridge (originally built by the Romans) crosses the Agueda where it runs through a steep gorge. This has extremely steep sides and the road on both sides zigzags down to the stone bridge, which is about 300 yards long and 15 feet wide. During late February there had already been a series of small actions between detachments of the 95th and French over possession of the village and the bridge. By 11 March the village was held by four companies under Lieutenant-Colonel Beckwith, with Captain Peter O'Hare's company acting as the outlying piquet on the hillside above the bridge. The hard service of performing outpost work had

The fateful bridge over the Agueda at Barba del Puerco. The French crossed the bridge from right to left before making their way up the hill by way of the goat track, visible on the opposite bank.
Ian Fletcher Battlefield Tours

taken its toll already and each company averaged only around 50 Rifleman.

General Fèrey, whose brigade of 3,000 men were stationed at San Felices, about two and a half miles to the east of the bridge, decided to attempt a surprise assault when he learnt from an informer that Beckwith's four companies numbered only some 200 men. As the night of 19 March was stormy with heavy rain and thick cloud cover, Fèrey chose it for his assault. Having assembled a volunteer force of some 600 *voltigeurs* and grenadiers as an assault force, and wearing their dark grey greatcoats over their uniforms, they advanced on the bridge. This elite 'forlorn hope' was backed up by some 1,500 infantry.

On the bridge, Captain O'Hare, accompanied by Lieutenant Simmons, posted sentries for the night at 8pm. Craufurd's *Standing Orders* had established the sensible practice of changing sentries at irregular intervals and at slightly varied positions. This night O'Hare placed a sergeant and 12 Riflemen about 50 yards from the bridge, positioning a double sentry behind a rock some 15 yards from the actual mouth of the bridge with orders to fire and fall back on the sergeant's party if attacked. The sergeant was ordered to hold his position as long as possible until reinforcements arrived. Meanwhile, Simmons crept across the bridge to the French side. Finding no sign of movement, Simmons returned, and took up residence in a tent that had been pitched on the hillside to allow the officer of the guard to have a little shelter from the elements between doing their rounds of the sentries. The rest of O'Hare's company, some 30 men, were fast asleep in a little church, whilst O'Hare himself, feeling unwell, retired to a nearby house, leaving his three subalterns to maintain the piquet.

At 11pm Lieutenants Mercer and Coane along with Simmons did their rounds of the sentries, but the combined noise of the water rushing under the bridge and the dampening effect of the heavy rain

meant the noise of Fèrey's approach was obscured. Thus a small group of *voltigeurs* was able to creep across the bridge and leap upon the two sentries, Riflemen Maher and McCann, without warning. Although bayoneted and captured, one managed to get off a warning shot, thus alerting the sergeant's piquet that was fortunately wide awake and ready for action. As the main French force charged across the bridge four-men abreast, the sergeant and his 12 men were able to open fire from behind their rocky position on the hillside whilst sending a runner back to the church. Although hopelessly outnumbered, the piquet slowly retreated up the very steep and rocky slope, maintaining its discipline even after the sergeant was shot, and exchanging fire with the *voltigeurs* as the latter attempted to deploy from the narrow entrance of the bridge and stumbled up the precipitous hillside.

Before the *voltigeurs* had ascended half-way up the slope, the remainder of the company under

The action on the Coa River at Almeida on 24 July 1810 saw the 95th, along with the rest of Craufurd's troops, perform magnificently in the face of overwhelming odds.

Lieutenant Mercer arrived and a furious exchange of fire began at distances as close as 15 yards. The rain had stopped and the moon began to emerge from behind the racing cloud cover. This was a very mixed blessing for the French for while it lit-up the hillside so they could more easily see their way, it also beautifully illuminated their white crossbelts against their dark greatcoats. This provided an excellent target for the Riflemen, whose black crossbelts and dark green uniforms ensured no such targeting assistance was offered. Utilising the rocks, these 40 Rifleman slowly gave ground for some 30 minutes whilst inflicting heavy losses on the advancing French as the latter progressively scrambled and gasped their way up. During this time Mercer was shot through the head and Simmons took command until O'Hare belatedly rushed up from his sickbed.

During this desperate action, the Riflemen often found themselves fighting with their sword bayonets as they attempted to contain the *voltigeurs* where the road emerged at the top of the hill. Simmons witnessed one brutal confrontation where a Rifleman placed the muzzle of his Baker against a French officer's head as he was leading a charge and blew the poor man's brains out, crying out as he did 'Revenge the death of Mr Mercer'. In his turn the Rifleman was riddled with at least seven

The joint training at Shorncliffe came into its own at the Coa, as soldiers of the 43rd, 52nd and 95th fought alongside each other, utilising all possible cover to delay the inexorable pressure of the French advance.

bullets by the *voltigeurs* following their officer. Yet Riflemen Green had an even more desperate story to relate that demonstrated the importance of the Riflemen's pairing. 'Three of these big ugly fellows came within 10 yards of me and my front-rank man. I had got my ball in my rifle, but had no time to return the ramrod, so both ball and ramrod went through one of them. My comrade fired, and the ball struck another in the breast. I threw my rifle down, as it was no use to me without a ramrod, and retired about 20 yards.' Green was then able to obtain a rifle from a wounded sergeant and maintain his position.

With a mixture of volleys and aimed fire poured upon them, O'Hare's men were inevitably pushed back. Yet before they were finally overwhelmed, Beckwith arrived at the head of two companies, his third having been detached to the right to prevent the French attempting an outflanking move. Seeing how serious the situation was, Beckwith led the 100 or so Riflemen forward in a charge, Simmons describing how they, having 'fixed swords came on like lions', and another bitter fight now ensued. Although some of the grenadiers managed to find their way up onto the right flank, Lieutenant James Stewart, the battalion Adjutant, with a small group of Riflemen, succeeded in driving them back, at one point the lieutenant having to fight off three Frenchmen at once.

The French, exhausted from their scramble up the slope and having lost a number of officers to aimed fire, now gave way despite their advantage in numbers and tumbled back down the dark and rocky slope. Beckwith led the three companies in pursuit, keeping them in extended formation in order to sweep the dispersed enemy back across the bridge. From the French side the main body of some 1,500 infantry fired blind volleys across the gorge to discourage any pursuit, this fire adding little but thick clouds of smoke to the already dark night but the distance and rocks ensured no further casualties were inflicted on the 95th.

***Opposite top**, Lieutenant-Colonel Thomas Sidney Beckwith, painted here in the full uniform of the 95th, was an inspired commander. His personal leadership ensured the bridge over the Coa was held open in the teeth of overwhelming French numbers, enabling Dawson's company of the 52nd to escape. Royal Green Jackets Museum*

***Opposite bottom**, the bridge over the Coa river, as seen from the French (or right) bank of the river. The Light Division was driven back across this bridge before forming up on the hill which towers above it. Ian Fletcher Battlefield Tours*

This classic outpost action was soon the talk of the Army, given that some 150 Riflemen (only three companies being engaged) had defeated 600 *voltigeurs* and grenadiers, and both Craufurd and Wellington wrote to congratulate Beckwith and his men. Fèrey's force lost over 100 men against 23 casualties on the British side. The latter's loss was disproportionate in that O'Hare's company lost one officer and five Riflemen dead and seven seriously wounded from an original strength of 53, against the two reserve companies who lost only two killed and eight wounded from just over 100. Needless to say, the action of Barba del Puerco justified the 95th's claim to be an élite. Throughout, the discipline showed by the men was superb regardless of the initial surprise, darkness and confusion, particularly the sergeant's piquet who continued to operate and display initiative even after their NCO was disabled. Although firing at night with a flintlock that blinded the shooter every time it was fired (as the powder in the flash-pan ignited), there was ample evidence of accuracy. At the bridgehead, several French corpses were found with numerous bullet wounds from the initial volley fired by the sergeant's piquet and most other French casualties were the result of bullets rather than the sword-bayonet.

As it was, Fèrey's attack had exposed the vulnerability of this position and a few days later

Beckwith was re-inforced by three companies drawn from the 43rd and 52nd. Shortly afterwards Craufurd decided the bridge was best covered by a cavalry vedette and Beckwith's force was moved to the fords at Villa de Ciervo, and replaced by troopers of the 1st Hussars of the KGL. However, if Barba Del Puerco was a severe challenge in terms of company-size outpost work, the next action was to see the whole Light Division put to a test upon which their very survival depended.

THE COA

Whilst the Light Division continued to perform its tasks with distinction after Barba del Puerco, by May a new French commander tasked with defeating Wellington, driving the British Army into the sea and capturing Lisbon had arrived: Maréchal André Massena. Given Massena could field over 65,000 men in the Army of Portugal even after detachments, Wellington was quite aware he could not hope to defeat this enemy host on the open battlefield. Rather, his plan was to delay Massena as long as possible on the frontier whilst a line of hopefully impregnable defences were constructed outside Lisbon, the Lines of Torres Vedras. The opening stages of Massena's offensive revolved around the fortresses of Ciudad Rodrigo and Almeida which guarded the northern route from

RIFLEMAN IN BATTLE

Spain into Portugal and which he had to capture. Having invested Ciudad Rodrigo in late June, the size of Massena's force ensured Wellington was powerless to aid its Spanish garrison who surrendered on 9 July. The Portuguese fort of Almeida was next, but to reach it Craufurd's Light Division, which was now posted along the River Coa, would have to be driven in. To perform this task, the legendary Maréchal Michael Ney and his 24,000-strong Sixth Corps, the largest in the Army of Portugal, was selected.

Craufurd was to do his men no favours in the decisions he took in the days leading up to 23 July. He still carried a psychological burden from the events of 1807 at Buenos Aires and bad luck had caused him to miss both Corunna and Talavera. He was still only a junior Brigadier-General whilst younger officers, such as William Beresford and Rowland Hill, were his seniors. Given his decisions of July 1810, it has been suggested Craufurd was determined to vindicate his reputation and demonstrate his abilities now he commanded the cream of Britain's light troops in a critical position. Yet matters had already gone poorly. Criticism of Craufurd had been voiced over the combat at Barquilla of 10 July where the less than expert handling of several squadrons of British and KGL light cavalry had permitted an exposed force of French foragers to escape before the supporting companies of the 95th could come up. Now Wellington, aware of the forthcoming French offensive, had urged Craufurd on 21 July to retreat across the Coa: '...I am not desirous of engaging in an affair beyond the Coa... would it not be better that you should come to this side with your infantry at least?' Yet Craufurd chose to cling to his precarious position with a river separating him from the rest of the army and only a single bridge across its rocky valley as an escape route! Now, his 4,000 men were about to confront 24,000 veterans under one of the French Army's most aggressive commanders. The events of

Opposite, **a Rifleman's view of the bridge over the Coa river. The French approached the bridge from the far end. This bridge was piled high with bodies after the fight.** *Ian Fletcher Battlefield Tours*

23 July would see the 95th (and the rest of the Light Division) tested to the extreme.

Craufurd, although he had faced both the Sixth and Eighth Corps of the Army of Portugal for over four and a half months along the Agueda, had never previously been approached by more than a single French division. Now, after a night of torrential rain, the first light of dawn on the 23rd found Ney advancing on the outlying piquets of the Light Division at the head of two cavalry brigades followed by three divisions of infantry in line of columns. Advancing down the road to Val de la Mula, Ney's cavalry immediately fell upon the outlying piquet consisting of Captain the Hon. John Stewart's company of the 95th and two guns, driving them back. The French troopers got amongst the retreating Riflemen and about 12 were captured. Before any further damage could be done, O'Hare's company was ordered forward to support Stewart's withdrawal and, taking up positions among some ruined walls, the Riflemen's aimed fire briefly checked the pursuit.

Both companies then retired upon the main position of the Light Division that had rapidly formed up some eight hundred yards to the right of Almeida, along the line of a rocky spur running parallel to the Coa. As the fortress of Almeida stood some two and a half miles from the Coa and the bridge, except for the far left of Craufurd's line, none of the fortress guns could be of assistance in any contest fought along this spur that ran all the way to the Coa. Craufurd, not realising the strength of Ney's assault, chose to hold his position rather than use the remaining time to effect a safe retreat. Craufurd must have also felt his position was strong, given the countryside was very broken and his front was covered by a series of high stone walls that provided excellent cover for the defence. From right to left, Craufurd deployed the 52nd with two of Ross's guns, while the centre was held by the 1st and 3rd *Caçadores*. The left of Craufurd's line was held by the 43rd and 95th, an ancient stone windmill denoting the far left being secured by a company of the 52nd.

Roughly an hour after driving in the outlying piquet, Ney launched a massive assault on the Light Division that not even its most intense volleys could hope to dent. As Simmons recorded: 'The enemy now advanced in vast bodies... the enemy's infantry formed line, and, with an innumerable multitude of skirmishers, attacked us fiercely.' Although driven back by the first fire, 'They came on again yelling, the drums beating.' Beckwith gave the order for the 95th to retire by half-companies and O'Hare withdrew part of his, leaving the other under Lieutenant Johnston to fend off the French.

During this delicate manoeuvre, Ney's columns charged forward and on the left a squadron of the Third Hussars swept from behind the walls of Almeida and fell upon the Riflemen. Catching O'Hare's men deployed in the open, they stood no chance and were cut to pieces in moments, 11 being killed and 45 captured (many of who were wounded). Only one officer (Simmons) and 11 men escaped, the former avoiding serious injury due to the 'large cloak rolled up and strapped across my body, and my haversack.' Meanwhile the remaining companies managed to find some shelter and the 43rd was able to drive back the main body of troopers with some well-aimed volleys, one of which killed the trooper who had captured Costello, enabling him (amongst others) to escape, albeit wounded in the right knee. In the ensuing confusion, small groups of *hussars* rode up and down the line-catching individual Riflemen and generally causing mayhem.

Now Craufurd realised the dire position he was in: his left was turned, his front was a sea of blue, while his right flank (and only escape route to the bridge) was threatened by further French columns. The road from Almeida to the bridge ran behind the length of Craufurd's position and there now followed a desperate rearguard action as the infantry attempted to hold back the tidal wave

of French to allow the cavalry, guns and baggage to escape. As Craufurd's line withdrew in echelon from the left, the 95th formed in small groups to either side of the road. But they were soon swamped by waves of *voltigeurs* described by Leach as 'swarms of bees' and as the situation descended into chaos and confusion, many parties of the 95th found themselves being 'hunted down like deer'. Despite all, the discipline and training of the 95th held, and whether led by an officer, an NCO or just a group of ordinary Riflemen, they obliged the *voltigeurs* to fight for every wall, rock and tree.

As they neared the bridge that was now choked with artillery caissons, guns, and horses, the 43rd, part of the 52nd and 95th made a brief stand on a knoll covered in fir trees, but the sheer weight of French troops proved too much and the knoll was successfully rushed. This left five companies of the 52nd trapped on the extreme right of the riverbank above the bridge. It was now that Beckwith and Major MacLeod of the 43rd placed themselves at the head of some 200 men of the 95th and 43rd and led them in a magnificent counter-attack to recapture the knoll. With fixed bayonets they swept the *voltigeurs* off the knoll and then held it for ten minutes against all comers, allowing the 52nd to escape across the bridge. Then, having made a final stand just above the bridge under a hail of fire, a last body of about 100 of the 43rd and 95th dashed back to the bridge. Leach, whose company it was, lyrically described this last method of retirement as 'skilter-Devil-take-the-hindmost.' Even then safety was delayed as Leach, both his fellow officers being wounded (one being the illustrious Harry Smith), found two artillery caissons unhitched in the middle of the bridge accompanied by a desperate officer of artillery. 'Our boys lined the battlements of the bridge keeping up a constant fire whilst he got his horses harnessed and got clear off.'

The fight was not quite over as Ney, convinced

he had so shaken the British and Portuguese they would flee if pushed, chose to launch an assault across the bridge. By now the men of the Light Division had already deployed to either side of the bridge, taking up defensive positions behind the rocks and walls, with Ross's guns placed across the road itself to sweep the mouth of the bridge. The first French assault undertaken by the *66eme Ligne* was shot to pieces, as was the next, a 300 strong *corps d'élite* of *chasseurs*. Finally, an exasperated Ney ordered a mounted staff officer to discover if the Coa could be forded. His fate was sealed as Riflemen shot him and his horse to death from their positions above the river. Ney had to accept the Light Division had escaped and called off any further assaults.

Losses were heavy, the Light Division's casualties coming to a total of 333. The 95th's share was one officer and 11 Riflemen killed, six officers, one sergeant and 54 Riflemen wounded (of whom two officers and a number of wounded Riflemen later succumbed), and one officer, one sergeant and 52 Riflemen 'missing', most of whom were actually prisoners. This total of 129 was only matched by the 43rd that had mostly fought alongside the 95th. On the French side, losses totalled 527 men of which four-fifths fell during Ney's reckless attempt to storm the bridge.

The Combat of the Coa must rate as one of the most difficult operations ever carried out by the 95th and the Light Division. Despite the overwhelming strength of the enemy, the battalion commanders had successfully performed a tactical withdrawal whilst in immediate physical contact with their opponents, saving the division's guns and baggage and leaving few prisoners. Whilst the soldiers were able to enjoy the admiration of the Army for this achievement, the events of the morning of 23 July were to add further to poor Craufurd's feeling of being 'unlucky' and the controversy that quickly arose was to haunt him till his dying day.

RIFLEMAN TRIUMPHANT

After the Coa, the Light Division was re-organised on 4 August into two brigades, the first under Beckwith consisting of four companies of the 95th (the right wing), the 43rd and the 3rd *Caçadores*. The second under Lieutenant-Colonel Barclay of the 52nd included his own regiment, the other four companies of the 95th (the left wing) and the 1st *Caçadores*. Meanwhile, the whole of the fifth battalion 60th remained divided up by company, providing a detachment of sharpshooters for each brigade. Whilst further units of Riflemen joined Wellington's Army, for example the three companies of Brunswick *Oels* armed and equipped as *Jäger* like the 60th, they were distributed as specialist marksmen. Thus two distinct roles had now clearly evolved as is reflected in these two modes of deployment. The detached companies of Riflemen, whether they were the 60th or the Brunswickers, answered to the commander of their respective brigade and essentially operated as marksmen. However, the first battalion 95th and later arrivals operated with the Light Division as a multi-purpose élite, utilised for just about every role

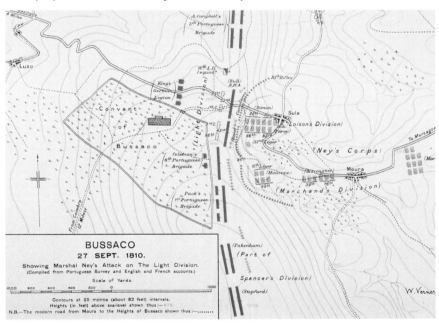

The battle of Bussaco on 27 September 1810 provided Craufurd's Light Division and the 95th in particular with a perfect opportunity to display their mastery of defensive/offensive linear tactics.

from skirmishing, scouting, screening, advance guards, rearguards, leading storming parties, through to providing a fire brigade role on the battlefield. The two subsequent battles of Bussaco and Fuentes de Oñoro, enabled Wellington's Riflemen to display most of these multiplicity of functions to the full.

At the battle of Bussaco, on 27 September 1810, the Riflemen of the 60th, 95th and *Caçadores* were deployed well down the steep slope that led up to the imposing ridge on which Wellington had chosen to make a stand. As each French assault went in, several of their officers subsequently recorded they had successfully broken through the first British line of defence, but this was of course nothing more than the deployed Riflemen waiting until the French assault was effectively on top of them before retiring on their main infantry support. The result: the screen of *voltigeurs* was effectively neutralised long before the main column came within range of the waiting artillery and infantry above. This indeed was the fate that awaited the first French assaults of the day led by Generals Merle and Heudelet, whose columns as they emerged just after 5.30am from the fog cloaking the valley below, met a determined resistance from companies of the 60th. Whilst the weight of the French assault ultimately enabled them to push up

the slope, the blast of artillery and musketry volleys, followed by a determined bayonet charge swept them back down. Even General Foy's partial success an hour later was soon repulsed.

Craufurd's Light Division gave a fine display of these tactics when their turn came at about 8.30am. They were placed on the left of Wellington's line with Pack's Portuguese brigade above the village of Sula to cover the main road to Coimbra. Craufurd deployed a very powerful line of Riflemen consisting of 750 men of the 95th, 650 of the 3rd *Caçadores* and some 60 selected Riflemen of the KGL alongside the 4th *Caçadores* placed by Pack. Positioned amongst the enclosures before Sula, this force of Riflemen confronted the assault of General Loison's Division of Ney's Corps. Loison's Division were in two columns, each consisting of six battalions; General Simon's brigade on the right, Férey's on the left, separated by some 200 yards. Each had a frontage of barely 120 yards, the men densely packed into columns of double-companies. Despite a strong screen of *voltigeurs* who quickly pushed through Sula, Craufurd's Riflemen poured in such a fire that Loison was obliged to re-inforce his skirmish line with several battalions of line troops, thus weakening his main assault force. Craufurd in turn re-inforced his own skirmish line with the 1st *Caçadores*, bringing his total force deployed as skirmishers to almost 2,000. Even with all three battalions of the *26eme Ligne* and *32eme Légér* similarly deployed, Loison could barely match them. Positioned on a knoll before Craufurd's main line was the battery of Captain Bull, which now also poured shot upon Loison's densely packed columns as they laboured forward up the steep, rock-strewn slope. All combined to ensure there was little to warn them of what lay in wait.

As intended, even as the Riflemen and gunners retired, the battalions of the 43rd and 52nd appeared to the exhausted and somewhat disorganised French to all but spring magically

Denis Dighton's contemporary painting of Riflemen skirmishing in the Peninsula, c.1811 shows how the green cord attached to the powder horn was loosened in action to enable the soldier to reload his rifle.

from the ground before them. In what some have described as the supreme moment in Craufurd's life, he was able dramatically to wave his men forward from the top of a rock, crying 'Now 52nd revenge the death of Sir John Moore! Charge, charge, Huzza!' This is indeed what they did. With the line of the 43rd and 52nd extending across the front and to either side of the column, some 1,800 British muskets first poured three volleys into Loison's men from barely 10 yards, before charging in and sweeping them back in utter chaos. George Napier of the 52nd described how 'Men, muskets, knapsacks and bayonets rolled down in one confused mass.' The Riflemen and *Caçadores*, who had meanwhile re-formed behind the 43rd and 52nd, followed on, subsequently maintaining a screen of skirmishers on the hillside to prevent any incursion by small bodies of French troops. For the loss of just 132 men, the Light Division had smashed Loison's brave troops and inflicted almost 1300 casualties.

On 3 April 1811 at Sabugal, Beckwith demonstrated the 95th's tremendous flexibility in combat, as well as his own fine leadership qualities, on the familiar banks of the Coa. As Wellington commenced the advance that ultimately led to the battlefield of Fuentes de Oñoro, the orders of the less than able General Erskine directed Beckwith's brigade to cross the Coa in a dense morning fog some two miles closer to Sabugal than ordered by Wellington. As Kincaid recorded, 'We instantly uncorked our muzzle-stoppers, off with our lock-caps, and our four companies of Riflemen led through the river (which was deep and rapid), followed by the 43rd, driving in the enemy's piquet which defended it.' Thanks to Erskine, instead of Beckwith working around the flank of General Merle's French division, he now ran straight into it. At that moment the fog cleared and Beckwith found he was confronted by over twice his own numbers. To make matters worse, a sudden downpour of rain rendered many rifles and muskets inoperative for a while. There followed a superb demonstration of what British light troops were capable of when Beckwith fell back to a low rise topped by a stone wall and proceeded first to defeat an assault by Merle's division and then, with the support of the rest of the division, fend off ever increasing numbers of French infantry and cavalry to drive forward. With the arrival of Major-General Thomas Picton's Third Division, only the intensifying downpour of rain caused Wellington to call off what was an otherwise victorious pursuit. It should be stressed that this display of aggressive tactics seeing the 95th and the rest of the Light Division switching back and forth between defensive and offensive moves, was achieved without Erskine who sat at the head of his cavalry doing nothing.

Whilst the French lost 61 officers and 689 men, the Light Division suffered just 143 casualties (total British and Portuguese losses were 179) of whom only 20 came from the two battalions of the 95th. As for Beckwith, he was the toast of the Army. Wellington wrote in his subsequent despatch: 'I consider the action that was fought by the Light Division, by Colonel Beckwith's Brigade principally, with the whole of the [French] IInd Corps, to be one of the most glorious that British troops were ever engaged in.' Kincaid, who at Sabugal appears to

This view from the Light Division's position at Bussaco, looking forward to the village of Sula where the 95th were initially deployed to meet the French assault gives an idea of the precipitous contours the French had to contend with. *Ian Fletcher Battlefield Tours*

have acted as Brigade-Major by Beckwith's side wrote in unashamed praise: '...he was just the man to grapple with any odds...Beckwith was the life and soul of the fray; he had been the successful leader of those who were then around him in many a bloody field and his calm clear commanding voice was distinctly heard amid the roar of battle, and cheerfully obeyed. He had but single companies to oppose to the enemy's battalions, but strange as it may appear I saw him twice lead successful charges with but two companies of the 43rd against an advancing mass of the enemy.' Furthermore, 'Beckwith's manner of command on these occasions was nothing more than a familiar sort of conversation with the soldier... seeing the necessity for immediate retreat, he called out, "Now, my lads, we'll just go back a little if you please." On hearing which every man began to run, when he shouted again, "No, no, I don't mean that – we are in no hurry – we'll just walk quietly back, and you can give them a shot as you go along." This was quite enough, and was obeyed to the letter.' It was thus keenly felt when a year later Beckwith's failing health forced him to return to England, never to return. Kincaid spoke for many when he wrote that the 'army lost one of the ablest of its outpost generals. Few officers knew so well how to make the most of a small force. His courage, coupled with his thorough knowledge of the soldier's character, was of that cool intrepid kind that would, at any time, convert a routed rabble into an orderly effective force. A better officer probably never led a brigade into the field!'

Beckwith's departure came on top of the death of Craufurd, who expired on 24 January 1812 from wounds received during the assault on the breach at Ciudad Rodrigo. After a brief interval under the interim leadership of Generals Bernard and Vandeleur, command of the Light Division passed to Major-General Charles von Alten with whom it remained until the conclusion of the Peninsular War. Under Alten, the Light Division

maintained the high standards established by Moore and Craufurd, and Wellington was able to retain his implicit trust in its abilities in outpost duties, on the battlefield and even for siege work. Memorably, during the investment of Badajoz in early 1812, the Riflemen of the 95th were relied upon to suppress French snipers from seriously disrupting the progress of digging the siege works. On 30 March, when the breaching battery began bombardment of the bastion of La Trinidad, the gunners came under an accurate sniping fire over a distance of some 300 yards from the covered-way. A number of the 95th were called up and they soon eliminated the French marksmen. A few days later, both Kincaid and Simmons described how an officer and 10 picked shots dug rifle pits during the night opposite a number of French guns that had been causing numerous casualties amongst the British gunners. After just an hour of daylight the Riflemen had silenced the French guns, and the embrasures through which they had been firing were blocked up with gabions and sandbags. Any subsequent attempt to remove the gabions was met by a series of well-placed shots.

It was during this episode that Simmons participated in a fine demonstration of marksmanship. A French officer, identified by the large cocked hat he placed on the wall, took

Opposite, although this painting of the moment Craufurd, standing on the rock, ordered the ranks of the 43rd and 52nd to charge at Busaco is highly stylised, it admirably conveys the spirit of the moment.

Although Simkin's illustration of the 85th decidedly foreshortened the range at which they would have skirmished with the opposing *voltigeurs*, it does convey the generality of such a scene.

position behind it and commenced demonstrating his skill as a marksman, his men handing him loaded muskets for him to fire. Simmons called over one of his men and had him rest his rifle on his left shoulder to gain the necessary elevation. They then both waited until the French officer was targeted from the flash of his musket, at which point he was apparently shot dead from some 250-300 yards, no further shots being received, although the cocked hat remained on the wall. Simmons bore something of a scar from this collaborative effort, the left side of his face having been immediately opposite the Baker's flashpan from which he received a nasty burn.

FINAL SUCCESS

At the battle of Vittoria in June 1813, the 95th demonstrated they had lost none of the somewhat reckless dash they had displayed from the first when they stormed the Bridge of Mendoza over the River Zadorra. Essentially the Rifles acted here more as an advanced assault force than sharpshooters. Despite this, Wellington described the Light Division in general under Alten as 'the flower of the army, the finest infantry in the world', an accolade well deserved after giving a splendid performance in the autumn of 1813 in the Pyrenees. For the Rifles, there was to be a

memorable demonstration of their skills and élan as the war drew to a close at the unique action at Tarbes on 20 March 1814. Here, all three battalions of the 95th fought together to crush twice their own number of French troops.

Following the victory at Orthez on 27 February, Wellington maintained the pressure on Maréchal Soult's Army as it retreated deeper into southern France. The latter was determined to fight one more rearguard action whilst the bulk of his army gained ground on Wellington's pursuit and he selected the position around the village of Tarbes for this. Rather than sacrifice soldiers to drive the French from a position they only intended to hold as a delaying tactic, Wellington chose to manoeuvre around the flanks to trigger a French retreat. It was whilst Major-General William Clinton was undertaking this movement that the only serious fighting took place between the 95th and General Harispe's brigade. The latter held a steep-sided hill thickly wooded and Alten selected the entire 95th for the assault. This ensured every diarist then serving with the regiment was involved; Costello, Kincaid, Simmons, Smith and Surtees all testify to it being a severe fight.

Deployed as a thick line of skirmishers, the third battalion on the right, the second in the centre and the first on the left, they moved forward into the trees and up the slope against determined French opposition. According to Surtees, as the Riflemen drove the screen of *voltigeurs* back towards the summit, '...we suffered considerably for they occupied the hedges and dikes on the high ground, from which it was necessary to dislodge them.' Having reached the summit, the Rifles found Harispe had thrown up earthworks on either side of a windmill that topped the hill and the 95th was forced to engage in a severe fire-fight. 'At length, after much smart skirmishing, we gained the height, but found the whole of their heavy infantry drawn up on a steep acclivity, near the windmill, which allowed them to have line behind line, all of which

As with all light infantry, French *voltigeurs* had to be adept at providing cover for a retreat as well as an assault.

***Opposite*, by 1813, the Rifles had the luxury of tents.**

could fire at the same time over each other's heads, like the tiers of guns in a three-decker.' This desperate fire-fight was conducted at ranges of less than 100 yards and only concluded when the French realised their position had been turned by Clinton. The need for personal leadership in such a contest was underlined by the heavy loss of officers as compared to rank and file, 11 of the former to 80 of the latter, almost 10% of those engaged.

Commenting on this remarkable action, as witnessed from the supporting line of the Light Division, Major John Blakiston, commanding a battalion of Portuguese *Caçadores*, left a sterling testament to the 95th Rifles at the conclusion of the Peninsular War (as reported by Kincaid). 'Nothing could exceed the manner in which the 95th set about the business...Certainly I never saw such skirmishers as the 95th...They could do the work much better and with infinitely less loss than any other of our best light troops. They possessed an individual boldness, a mutual understanding, and a quickness of eye, in taking advantage of the ground which, taken altogether, I never saw equalled. They were as much superior to the French *voltigeurs*, as the latter were to our skirmishers in general. As our regiment was often employed in supporting them, I think I am fairly qualified to speak of their merits.'

WATERLOO

When Napoleon abdicated in April 1814, all three battalions serving with Wellington returned home. The third battalion almost immediately embarked for America, whilst the first and second remained in garrison in England. The only Riflemen left on the Continent were four companies in the Netherlands under Lieutenant-Colonel Alexander Cameron, a veteran of the original Experimental Rifle Corps. These companies, one each from the first and second battalions and two from the third battalion, fought in the closing stages of the war at the abortive sieges of Bergen-op-Zoom and Antwerp.

Top, Vittoria, 21 June 1813. The bridge over the Zadorra at Tres Puentes. Kempt's brigade of the Light Division, including the first and third battalions of the 95th, crossed the bridge from left to right before advancing on to the knoll of Iruna, from which this view was taken. *Ian Fletcher Battlefield Tours*

Bottom, Tarbes, 20 March 1814. The 95th advanced from out of the trees on the left. The fight at Tarbes was considered by many veterans to have been the sharpest action of the war. *Ian Fletcher Battlefield Tours*

Given the nature of siege warfare, the sharpshooter skills of the Riflemen were at a premium and it was during Bergen-op-Zoom that a particularly well-known duel took place between a Rifleman of the 95th and a French *voltigeur*.

Each took up their respective firing positions behind two trees some one hundred yards apart and proceeded to pot away. Proving that the Baker rifle was not capable of performing miracles, after several shots both combatants were unwounded. The emphasis in the 95th, however, on individual initiative now paid off as the Rifleman, unable to obtain a clear shot without running the risk of being hit by his smoothbore-armed opponent, switched to cunning.

Transfixing a loaf of bread on the end of his sword-bayonet, he stuck this out from behind the tree and the *voltigeur* immediately proved his ability with a musket by putting a ball clean through. Pretending he had been hit, the Rifleman now rolled about on the ground as if critically hit and the Frenchman, never one to miss an opportunity for a spot of looting, dashed forward from cover. Moments later he fell dead from his victim's rifle.

Having remained in the Netherlands into the opening months of 1815, these veteran Riflemen found themselves perfectly placed when, after Napoleon's escape from Elba, Wellington began assembling his multi-national army around Brussels.

J.D. Aylward's famous painting *The Morning of Waterloo*, captures the moment Wellington shared breakfast with the 95th.
Royal Green Jackets Museum

Six companies of the first battalion and five of the second ultimately joined them, thus giving Wellington just over two battalions of British Riflemen. By early May, Wellington had organised the British element into brigades and divisions. Rather than placing detachments of the 95th with each, he created a light brigade under Major-General Frederick Adam composed of the 52nd, 71st, and the six companies of the second battalion (674 officers and men) and the two companies of the third battalion 95th (214 officers and men). Equally, the seven companies of the first battalion 95th (656 officers and men) formed part of Major-General Sir James Kempt's Brigade.

The 95th were not the only Riflemen in Wellington's Army, there being two companies of Brunswick *Jäger*, the rifle-armed elements of the KGL, and two companies of Hanoverian Field *Jäger*, both formations containing a number of Peninsular veterans. The two Brunswick companies of *Gelernte Jäger* formed half of the Avant-Garde Battalion of sharpshooters, the other two companies being light infantry. There were two light battalions of the KGL at Waterloo (each some 450 men strong), the 2nd under Major George Baring famously defending the farm of La Haye Sainte. In each battalion there was only a single élite sharpshooter company armed with

the Baker rifle whilst the remainder were armed with standard light infantry muskets. Equally, in both the KGL and Hanoverian line battalions, each light company had selected *Scharfschutzen* armed with Bakers, with up to a third of each light infantry company armed with rifles. This mixing of Riflemen and light infantry in the same battalion ironically harked back to the original 1801-03 ideas of having a certain proportion of standard light infantry battalions armed with rifles. Thus the Brunswick, KGL and Hanoverian *Jäger* operated as only elements of an otherwise generalised light infantry and line battalions providing a select number of specialist marksmen. Only the two companies of Hanoverian Field *Jäger* (some 331 officers and men) under Captain von Reden could be said to match the 95th in terms of being designated to operate independently from any parent formation.

Only the first battalion of the 95th under Lieutenant-Colonel Sir Andrew Barnard fought at Quatre Bras on 16 June, operating on the left of Wellington's line. Here they spent much of the afternoon functioning as light infantry, first clearing the Bois des Cérises (Cherry Wood) of French *voltigeurs* then assisting the rest of Kempt's brigade to push Bachelu's troops back across the fields. This service was performed at a cost, the 656 officers and men of the battalion suffering 67 casualties, some 10% of those engaged. The following day they performed the duty of rearguard in the pouring rain, retiring with the British cavalry through Genappe and over the River Dyle to the ridge before Waterloo where they went into bivouac just behind La Haye Sainte Farm.

The following day, 18 June, witnessed the elements of all three battalions of the 95th operating in just about every conceivable role possible as Wellington's men fought ever more desperately against the French onslaught. Operating as coherent battalion formations rather than detached companies of sharpshooters, they often had to serve as line infantry. This was particularly true, and rather ironic given their

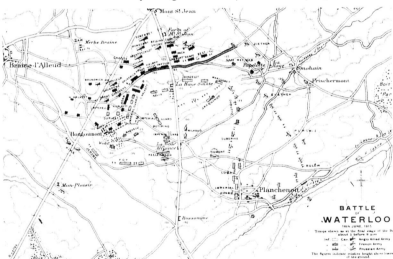

The battle of Waterloo saw elements of all three battalions of the 95th, plus sundry German units of Riflemen play a major role in Wellington's victory.

parent brigade's expected function, for the eight companies of the second and third battalions in General Adam's light brigade deployed to the rear of Hougoumont on Wellington's right. The brigade formed up by battalion, the 52nd on the right, 71st in the centre, with the two companies of the third battalion 95th and the second battalion 95th on the left. It was only late in the afternoon, around four o'clock, that they went into action for the first time, both the 95th and 71st deploying forward, with the 52nd in reserve to counter a thick screen of *voltigeurs* advancing upon Hougoumont who were supported by well-directed French guns.

As both the 71st and 95th were formed in a close-order four-deep line due to the presence of French cavalry in the vicinity and the need to be ready to form square, casualties were heavy. Rifleman John Lewis of the second battalion recalled: 'My first-rank man was wounded by part of a shell through his foot, and he dropped as we was advancing. I covered the next man I saw, and had not walked twenty steps before a musket-shot came sideways and took his nose clean off, and then I covered another man, which was the third. Just after that the man stood next to me on my left had his left arm shot off by a nine-pound shot just above the elbow and he turned round and caught hold of me with his right hand, and

the blood ran all over my trousers. We was advancing and he dropped directly!' When the two regiments finally came upon a body of French infantry, a severe exchange of fire took place. Captain William Eales of the third battalion 95th recorded: 'I can only here observe that the French and 71st were closer than I ever before saw any regular formed adverse bodies, and much nearer than troops usually engage.' Although the bulk of the French were driven back into the smoke by the weight of British fire, Eales records launching a bayonet charge with his company to drive off one group situated in a small depression in a rye field. At no point during this advance did the 95th deploy as skirmishers or act as sharpshooters, rather they fought as line infantry.

Shortly after the 52nd moved up to join the 71st and 95th on the forward slope alongside Hougoumont, the massed cavalry charges of the afternoon commenced. The second battalion 95th formed battalion square alongside their red-coated comrades on the left of the brigade, whilst the two companies of the third battalion fought with the 71st. As before, the Riflemen do not appear to have utilised the extended range or accuracy of their Bakers. Rather Eales records that he 'kept every man from firing until the Cuirassiers approached within 30 or 40 yards of the Square, when I fired a

The King's German Legion provided Wellington with some of his finest troops. Although Knoetel's drawing of the 1st battalion KGL Light Infantry shows them as clothed and equipped as Riflemen, only one in 10 were so armed.

The 2nd battalion KGL Light Infantry formed the garrison of La Haye Sainte under the command of Major Baring. As with the 1st battalion, only one in 10 were armed with rifles.

Next page, The sand pit at Waterloo, 18 June, 1815. Just after 1.30pm the main French infantry assault of the day under General D'Erlon swept towards Wellington's centre and the Ohaine crossroads. The key to this position was the farm of La Haye Sainte, its garrison consisting of Major George Baring's 2nd Light Battalion of the KGL, supported to its flank and rear by the first battalion of the 95th Rifles.

Illustrated here is the moment the column of General Bourgeois' brigade of infantry, fronted by a thick screen of *voltigeurs*, assailed the gentle slope leading to the Ohaine road, supported to their rear by Travers' *cuirassiers*. To Bourgeois' left, the infantry of General Quiot's brigade swarm around the walls of La Haye Sainte attempting to break in. Ahead, the Riflemen of Captains Leach and Chawner are evacuating the sandpit, covered by the fire of Captain Johnston's company, defending the knoll to their rear, whilst the 1st Light Battalion of the KGL covers their exposed flank. The Brussels road to their left runs into a deep cut between banks some 15 to 20 feet high, blocked by two impromptu barricades. Captain Hew Ross's RHA battery stands to the rear of the farm, two of whose guns are placed in the road. Behind the thorn hedge lining the Ohaine Road are the Riflemen of Captains Beckwith, Glasse and Lee. On the reverse slope, the serried ranks of Kempt's brigade await Picton's order to counter-attack. *Painting by Christa Hook.*

volley from my Company which had the effect, added to the fire of the 71st, of bringing so many horses and men at the same moment to the ground, that it became quite impossible for the Enemy to continue their charge.' Equally, along with the rest of the troops in square, in between pouring volleys into the serried ranks of *cuirassiers*, the 95th had to contend with artillery fire tearing through their ranks between charges, a number of French horse artillery pieces coming within 150 yards and hammering the Riflemen with grapeshot. Even the French horsemen inflicted casualties, Rifleman Lewis relating how some troopers fired their carbines into the densely packed walls of the square, the man on his right being shot through the stomach, 'falling back like a pig stuck in the throat.' Lewis himself had a lucky escape when another carbine shot struck his rifle as he was loading it, breaking the stock and bending the barrel. Lewis was soon able to replace his loss when his sergeant, Thomas Pilling, was sliced in two by a cannon ball, leaving his rifle undamaged. So severe were the losses that, as the cavalry assaults petered out in the early evening, Lewis' battalion was left under the command of a junior captain, Joseph Logan, who was only slightly wounded, the latter describing how the battalion was 'cruelly mauled with shot and shell'.

Even at the climax of the battle, the companies

of the 95th with Adam still had no opportunity to act as skirmishers. Given that French infantry occupied the hedge line running alongside Hougoumont flanking Adam's line, he pulled his brigade back behind the ridge, thus also gaining shelter from the cannon balls that were still falling in profusion. It was whilst the brigade was gaining its breath on the reverse slope that Napoleon launched forward elements of his Imperial Guard in a final assault. As Adam advanced over the ridge to confront this, the hordes of French skirmishers moving ahead of the Guard poured a destructive fire into the ranks of the 95th. Due to the still active presence of various groups of French horsemen, the 95th had to remain in close order formation, casualties becoming even higher as French horse artillery came up and opened fire with grapeshot. Nonetheless, all three of Adam's regiments stood their ground and were rewarded by the sight of the serried ranks of the Imperial Guard emerging from the smoke as their skirmishers fell back.

With the 52nd now formed as the left of Adam's line, with the 95th in the centre and 71st on the right, they combined to hammer the Guard from less than 50 yards with a hail of volley fire. Although unable to reload as fast as their Brown Bess-armed colleagues, at this range the balls from the Baker rifles must have almost all found a recipient! As history records, the Imperial Guard withered under the sheer weight of fire, not even the bravest troops being proof against such a wall of lead. As the Guard was forced back, Adam's men advanced across the shallow valley and only now were several companies of the 95th able to deploy as skirmishers to cover the front of the 71st. Captain Logan claimed that Wellington himself accompanied the Riflemen, urging them to 'Move on, my brave fellows!' As it was, the complete collapse of Napoleon's Army, combined with the sheer exhaustion of Adam's men meant they soon came to rest amongst the French dead and wounded, seizing many of the guns that had been pelting them with cannon shot all afternoon.

Another rifle-armed unit was the Brunswick *Jäger*, here deployed behind cover to pick off key personnel amongst the approaching French troops.

It was a somewhat different battle for the first battalion of the 95th, who were able to operate in a manner reminiscent of their original brief as sharpshooters. They were deployed from the start in and around the sandpit and crossroads in the centre of Wellington's position to cover the front of their parent brigade. The regimental staff with Colonel Barnard, along with three reserve companies under Captains Lee, Beckwith and Glasse, took position behind the Ohaine Road and to the left of the Brussels road. 150 yards forward of the Ohaine road at a knoll fronted by a hedge, Captain Johnston formed his company. Finally, beyond this hedge at the foot of the knoll was a sandpit between four-five yards deep and roughly 50 by 100 yards across dug into the bank of the Brussels road (as this entire area was deeply excavated to build the Lion Mount some years later, a precise description is impossible). Here the two remaining companies of Captains Leach and

Chawner took position under the command of the former. Major Baring garrisoned the farm of La Haye Sainte itself with the 2nd Light Battalion of the KGL. The Brussels road running between the farm and sandpit was barricaded, although its construction was of questionable integrity.

Unlike their colleagues behind Hougoumont who saw little of the battle until late afternoon, the first battalion had a grandstand seat from the very beginning, the main French lines being barely 500 yards to their front. Aimed at Wellington's troops formed to their rear, various cannon balls from the opening French bombardment around 11am fell short, thus causing the first casualty to the 95th when a Rifleman lost his head. This ensured most lay prone for several hours whilst lumps of iron flew overhead. Shortly after 1.30pm, the massed ranks of General D'Erlon's Corps, some 18,000 men in four divisions formed up in a close-packed column of divisions by battalion, lumbered forward, its front

Companies of the second and third battalions of the 95th were obliged to form square to meet the waves of French *cuirassiers* that swept over Wellington's right wing during the afternoon. Whilst this Victorian painting conveys the drama of the experience, it is highly unlikely the Riflemen continued to wear their backpacks or that the *cuirassiers* were able to approach to almost sword length.
Ian Fletcher Battlefield Tours

covered by the equivalent of an entire brigade of skirmishers. It was General Quiot's Division (who commanded in the absence of General de Vaux) that bore down on La Haye Sainte and the Ohaine/Brussels crossroads. Sheltered in the sandpit, Leach and Chawner waited until the *voltigeurs* were barely 100 yards distant before they rose and cut a swathe through the French skirmish line. With Captain Johnston's men on the knoll adding to the carnage, and flanking fire from La Haye Sainte, the *voltigeurs* were halted whilst the column they were screening, General Bourgeois' brigade (*28eme* and *105eme Ligne*), was forced to incline to the right.

Seeing the pressure the 95th were under, Wellington sent forward the 1st Light Battalion of the KGL who formed line to the left of Johnston's position. General Quiot's brigade (*54eme* and *55eme Ligne*), having overrun the orchard of La Haye Sainte, was now lapping around its walls whilst Bourgeois' brigade regained its equilibrium and pressed on against the sandpit and knoll. With a second French division under General Donzelot coming up on their left, the three advanced companies and the KGL, rather than be overrun, fell back across the Ohaine Road on the three reserve companies. This retirement was not completed before, according to Kincaid, 'some of our officers and theirs had been engaged in personal

combat.' Once back behind the Ohaine Road, due to the wounding of Colonels Barnard and Cameron, command had fallen to the senior captain, Henry Lee, and in the tense and confused situation he mistakenly ordered the three reserve companies to retire. Fortunately Kincaid, who as battalion adjutant was mounted and was thus aware of the actual orders issued by General Kempt 'that I would never quit that spot', corrected the situation and prevented a critical gap opening up just as the French assault broke upon the main line.

As Kincaid described it: 'When the heads of their columns showed over the knoll which we had just quitted, they received such a fire from our first line, that they wavered, and hung behind it a little; but, cheered and encouraged by the gallantry of their officers, who were dancing and flourishing their swords in front, they at last boldly advanced to the opposite side of our hedge, and began to deploy.' All six companies and the KGL were able to pour a destructive fire into the packed ranks of Quiot and Donzelot's men, knocking over officers and drummers in particular, critically disrupting their attempt to deploy into line. Consequently, although the weight of the French took them onto the Ohaine road, they were caught partially deployed between column and line when Picton's Division, followed by the Union and Household cavalry brigades fell upon them. As D'Erlon's assault collapsed in chaos, the 95th and KGL followed up as far as the knoll and sandpit, resuming their original positions. All in all, this had been an almost textbook display of marksmanship and light infantry tactics.

Thoughts of victory were short-lived as a hail of French shot began falling on and around their position. Then, around 3.30pm, the 95th and KGL had to contend with a renewed infantry assault by elements of Quiot's and Bachelu's Divisions. As their target was the farm, the 95th found they were dealing with ever-growing clouds of *voltigeurs* rather than a direct infantry attack. As French skirmishers skirted past to the left of the sandpit they reached the hedges

The first battalion 95th spent much of the day deployed along the hedges bordering the Ohaine Road and topping the knoll alongside La Haye Sainte.

Opposite, their ammunition having run out, the KGL, defending the now burning La Haye Sainte, used just their bayonets in a final desperate bid to repel the French.

bordering the Ohaine road, causing Wellington to pull his main line back a little. Mistaking this as the beginning of a retreat, Ney triggered the massed cavalry charges that saw the cream of the French heavy cavalry squandered. Sheltered by the hedges and sandpit, the companies of the first battalion 95th found themselves spectators to the drama unfolding to their right as regiment after regiment of *cuirassiers*, dragoons and even the cavalry of the Imperial Guard swirled around Wellington's squares. The few French horsemen who came the Rifles' way either fell victim to their Bakers or plummeted down the steep banks of the Brussels road.

As early evening came on and the French charges finally petered out, Maréchal Ney fed in more infantry in a determined effort to capture the farm and finally pierce Wellington's centre. An epic struggle now took place as Baring's men in the farm ran out of ammunition and were overwhelmed, only 43 escaping, whilst *voltigeurs* brought the sandpit under *enfilade* from both flanks. The two companies in the sandpit had no option but to fall back on Johnston's position on the knoll, then all three retreated to the reserve line behind the Ohain road. Due to high officer casualties, command now fell to Captain Leach, who had to contend with two French guns being brought up behind La Haye Sainte and pouring grapeshot into the ranks of the 95th. At this moment the range and accuracy of the Baker rifle, not to mention the marksmanship of the 95th, came into its own. Whilst the guns were beyond the range of the Brown Bess, within minutes most of the gunners had fallen to the Baker and the guns were silenced.

There followed a prolonged exchange of fire at ranges of less than 80 yards lasting over two hours as Leach's Riflemen successfully pinned down the French troops now occupying the sandpit and knoll. It was during this period the 95th had the agonising view of both the 5th and 8th battalions of the KGL being sacrificed by the stupidity of the Prince of Orange. Ordered forward in line despite the

Opposite, **as the French swept around the walls of La Haye Sainte, they discovered one of its gates had been chopped up for firewood the previous night and was inadequately barricaded, leaving the KGL to fight it out at bayonet point.**

obvious body of French *Carabiniers* hovering nearby, the Riflemen could do nothing to save the Hanoverians as they were cut to pieces, mixed as they were with horsemen. Meanwhile, the few attempts that were made by the French infantry to push forward were repulsed by the 95th and KGL every time they advanced out of the growing gloom and dense smoke, albeit at a steady loss to the defenders. As Kincaid commented in respect of this period: 'I had never yet heard of a battle in which everybody was killed; but this seemed likely to be an exception, as all were going by turns.' This continued until just after 7pm when the drama of the final assault by the Imperial Guard was played out on the right. As the Guard retired so did their compatriots around La Haye Sainte and the surviving Riflemen under Leach pushed forward at Wellington's express order, driving the disintegrating French units back until darkness and exhaustion brought them to a halt some two miles behind the battlefield.

As 18 June drew to a close, the roll was taken in each company and the cost to the 95th of playing their part in defeating Napoleon quickly emerged. Of the 61 officers who had taken the field back at the commencement of the campaign, five were dead and 39 wounded, many critically. As for the original 1245 rank and file, no less than 108 were dead, 420 wounded and 27 missing. Overall, the 15 companies of the regiment present had suffered 46% casualties in just three days of fighting, the vast majority in just a few short hours during the afternoon and early evening of the 18th. When the survivors formed up the next morning, many companies were commanded by junior subalterns whilst all three battalions were led by captains, the first under Leach, the second Logan and the third Eeles, all three suffering from minor wounds. By 10am on the 19th, the various companies of the 95th had commenced the march to Paris with their brigades, which they entered with the Army on 7 July. The Napoleonic Wars were over.

RIFLEMAN LEGACY

Opposite, although the cut and general design of the uniform of the 60th King's Royal Rifle Corps changed with prevailing fashion (as seen here in the mid-1820s), the sergeant's short-tailed jacket retained its distinctive red facings and three rows of silver buttons.

THE RIFLE BRIGADE

During the course of the Napoleonic Wars, the 95th Rifles had been used as a multi-purpose élite rather than just specialist sharpshooters. This latter role had fallen to the fifth battalion 60th Royal Americans and other smaller bodies of Riflemen distributed throughout the Army. The reality of the 95th's function was recognised in 1816 as it was removed from the line and its three battalions styled 'The Rifle Brigade'. Consequently the emphasis on marksmanship declined somewhat, and the multi-purpose role was highlighted, the Rifle Brigade being dispatched on various colonial duties around the globe. Whilst the second battalion and third battalions returned from France in 1816, the first battalion did not return until October 1818, the third battalion being in turn reduced the following year. Subsequently the first battalion served in Canada, the Mediterranean and then the Cape before returning to England in 1853. The second battalion saw service in Portugal, the Mediterranean, Bermuda and finally Canada, whence it returned to England in 1852.

Whilst the bulk of the Army were still armed with smoothbore muskets, between 1838-40 the Rifle Brigade received an expensive replacement for its veteran Bakers, the Brunswick Rifle. It was not a successful weapon. For many years there had been considerable criticism of the Baker's angular seven-groove rifling proving to be less accurate than other forms of rifling and more easily fouled. Many German and privately-made weapons had eleven-groove rifling with rounded grooves and a twist of from one-half to one full turn in the length of the barrel that made for ease of loading, greater accuracy and less fouling. Yet when George Lovell, a leading gunsmith, was tasked by the Board of Ordnance to experiment to identify the best option, he came up with a new rifle, which had a two-groove system using a patched, belted ball.

The ordinary Rifleman rapidly discovered the Brunswick shared most, if not all, the undesirable faults of the Baker. It was recorded in 1852 that 'The force required to ram down the ball being so great as to render a man's hand much too unsteady for accurate shooting'. Within 10 years of its issue, there was a rising chorus expressing dissatisfaction with its performance. It was to be the last specialist muzzle-loading rifle issued, for in January 1853 the Rifle Brigade were ordered to exchange their Brunswicks for the Army's new standard long arm, the Pattern 1851 Rifle-musket, often referred to as the Enfield Rifle. Rather than offering any radical development in rifling, the new musket utilised a revolution in terms of the basic conception of ammunition: the cylindro-conoidal expanding bullet, the Minié system. Although this rifle's backsight was rather optimistically graduated to 1000 yards, it was certainly capable of aimed fire to between 400-500 yards, effectively double that of either the Baker or Brunswick rifles.

Armed with this new rifle, both battalions of the Rifle Brigade were landed in the Crimea in 1854. Here the British Army fielded a Light Division and the general assumption was that the nature of the conflict would be broadly similar to that of the Peninsular and Waterloo campaigns. Certainly the Rifle Brigade were detailed to act as sharpshooters and skirmishers as required. At the battle of the Alma, they deployed as a line of skirmishers as the British Army assaulted across the shallow River Alma and up the slope of the Kourgane against the heavily defended Great Redoubt. Whilst the Rifle Brigade seemed to have retained its original function at the Alma, it was in fact the last time they ever acted as such in a major battle. With most of the Army equipped with Enfield rifles, the subsequent battle of Inkerman and the long siege of Sebastopol proved all troops could act as skirmishers and sharpshooters and thus the Rifle Brigade's role as specialist marksmen vanished by 1856.

KING'S ROYAL RIFLE CORPS

At the conclusion of the Peninsular War, the 60th was still very much a 'foreign' regiment with around half its rank and file being German, along with significant

numbers of French, Italian and Dutch, and its orders were still given in German. In mid-1815, the 60th was reduced to just two battalions, the fifth 'jäger' battalion being one of those disbanded, its men being dispatched to the second battalion based at Quebec. In 1818, the two red-coated battalions re-clothed into the green, scarlet-faced uniforms previously worn by the old fifth battalion. One battalion was armed with Baker rifles whilst the other carried light infantry muskets. In 1824, all remaining 'foreign' soldiers were drafted out of the regiment and it dropped the title 'The Royal American Regiment' to become the 60th (Duke of York's Rifle Corps and Light Infantry). Very soon after its title was changed to the 60th (Duke of York's Own Rifle Corps), it changed again in 1830 to the 60th (King's Royal Rifle Corps), both battalions still carrying Baker rifles. Like the Rifle Brigade, they were utilised for general colonial duties, seeing service in Canada, the Mediterranean and the Cape. Also like the Rifle Brigade, the 60th KRRC were re-equipped by 1840 with the Brunswick and by 1854 with the Enfield. It is interesting to note that battalions of both the 60th KRRC and Rifle Brigade were chosen to fight in the Cape in the early 1850s, it being felt such troops were still suitable for the sort of dispersed bush fighting such campaigns involved.

In 1857, battalions of both the 60th KRRC and Rifle Brigade helped suppress the Indian Mutiny, after which there was a return to general colonial service. Amongst the many colonial campaigns of the late Victorian period, various battalions of the Rifle Brigade saw action during the Ashanti Expedition of 1874, the First Afghan War 1878-80, the Nile Expedition of 1884, the Third Burma War 1885-87, Egypt in 1898 and then the Second Boer War 1899-1902. Separate battalions of the 60th KRRC fought in China 1860, the Red River Expedition of 1870, the Afghan Campaigns of 1870-80, the Zulu War of 1879 and finally the First Boer War of 1881.

The general expansion of the British Army to meet the demands of the Crimean War saw a third battalion of the 60th KRRC re-raised, the fourth being re-raised in 1857 to help meet the demands of the Indian Mutiny (as was a fourth battalion of the Rifle Brigade). The Cardwell reforms of 1881 saw the '60th' finally dropped and the regiment officially became the 'King's Royal Rifle Corps'. In memory of her recently deceased husband, in 1862 Queen Victoria decreed it should become 'The Prince Consort's Own (Rifle Brigade)', but in 1881 Cardwell had its title reversed to 'The Rifle Brigade (The Prince Consort's Own)'. By now only the green uniforms, badges and traditions remained of their original purpose. In all other respects both the King's Royal Rifle Corps and Rifle Brigade were ordinary infantry regiments. However, the high standards, be it in drill, dress or discipline remained, both regiments being considered highly fashionable for an aspiring officer, being effectively just one step below the Guards in terms of 'social' ranking.

Much the same occurred in other armies that already boasted established *Jäger* regiments. In both the Prussian and Austrian armies, *Jägers* continued to command respect, with regiments being included in the Prussian Royal Guard. Like their British offspring, as the century progressed and all infantry came to be armed with rifled weapons, their specialist sharpshooter and skirmisher roles became part of unit history. However, in terms of uniform and designation, *Jäger* battalions continued to be trained and utilised as multi-purpose formations, able to perform scouting duties alongside taking their place in the line when called upon. As late as 1914, German *Jäger* battalions were designated to scout ahead of major formations, reporting back on enemy positions, troop concentrations and seizing strategic locations such as bridges and the like.

DIARISTS OF THE 95th
The years after Waterloo proved an anti-climax for all ranks. For many rank and file, the spiritual traumas

Top, by 1900, the silver device officers of the King's Royal Rifle Corps wore on their pouch-belt bore the name of every major battle the regiment had fought in. **Bottom,** a similar silver device was worn by officers of the Rifle Brigade on their pouch-belts, albeit listing different glories.

and physical stress of years of hard campaigning meant many were rapidly discharged to fend for themselves as civilians. For the officers, the immediate post-war reductions in the 60th and of the third battalion of the Rifle Brigade in 1819, meant many were either placed on half-pay or faced years of mundane service with little hope of promotion. A classic example was William Humbley, who, having joined the 95th as a subaltern in 1807, subsequently served at Copenhagen, then in every battle in the Peninsular from Roliça through to Toulouse, then finally at Quatre Bras and Waterloo. During this remarkable span of service he was wounded five times, including a matching musket ball in each shoulder. Despite all this, when the third battalion was disbanded he was placed on the half-pay list, to survive on what was little more than a pittance. Yet 35 years later, aged 62, Humbley was recalled to the colours during the Crimean War!

The long decades following 1815 provided a good opportunity for many Riflemen to commit their rich range of wartime experience to paper. As many subsequent writers have noted, the 95th was unique in producing such a plethora of memoirs for the relatively short period of its Peninsular and Waterloo service. This has been partially explained by the superior standard of soldier who was originally recruited into the corps. It also had much to do with the determination of a few officers, who urged their compatriots to commit their memories to paper, in some cases personally assisting less literate rankers by recording their verbal accounts. Although such an exercise is common today, for the era of the early 19th century it was unique.

The first of the accounts to be published was that of John Kincaid. William Napier had commenced publishing his *History of the Peninsular War* in 1827 (it ultimately ran to five volumes), thus triggering a wave of interest in the conflict. This seems to have encouraged Kincaid (who had remained a serving officer in the 95th, being promoted to captain in

1826), to write and publish *Adventures in the Rifle Brigade* in 1830. Kincaid's entertaining memoirs were well received which in turn encouraged Jonathan Leach to produce possibly the most detailed of the various accounts. He had originally entered the Army as an ensign in the 70th Foot in 1801, being subsequently appointed to the 95th as a captain in May 1806. He served throughout the Peninsular and Waterloo campaigns, being made a brevet-major in 1813 for distinguished service at Vittoria and a brevet-lieutenant-colonel in 1815 for his actions at Waterloo. Having been promoted to the substantive rank of major in October 1819, he retired in 1821. Leach maintained a diary throughout the war, each volume of which he dispatched home for safekeeping. Having retired, he used these as his primary source for his *Rough Sketches in the Life of an Old Soldier.*

The popularity of Kincaid and Leach's work ensured many others followed, particularly as so many veterans were now 'enjoying' their retirement, voluntary or otherwise. In 1833 William Surtees' memoirs were published, *Twenty-Five Years in the Rifle Brigade*, he having retired as quartermaster of the second battalion in 1826 due to ill health, only to die in 1830. Surtees' posthumously published memoirs were followed in 1835 by Kincaid's second work, *Random Shots from a Rifleman*. It was now that the accounts by various rankers began to appear, the first being Edward Costello's *Adventures of a Soldier* in 1841. Having been discharged from the Army in 1819, Costello spent a number of years as a civilian. In 1836 he had been appointed a captain in the British Auxiliary Legion, engaged in the Carlist War in Spain in support of the infant Queen Isabella. Having been wounded in action, he soon returned to England, subsequently managing to gain an appointment as a yeoman warder at the Tower of London. Like so many other veterans, he then used his effective retirement as an opportunity to commit his experiences to paper.

The next published account came in 1848 from

Below from left to right.

1 & 2. Apart from minor changes in the dimension and fittings of the bell-topped shako, the sergeant and Rifleman's uniforms remained essentially unaltered by 1842.

3. It was likewise for officers who, for full dress, continued to adopt affectations from the light cavalry as illustrated by this individual, c.1816, with gold lacing on his breeches.

4. A slightly more practical look could be affected by switching to grey overalls and buttoning the lapels across. Again showing the officers' uniform c.1816, it should be noted officers wore a double-breasted coat with round cuffs identical in cut to the rest of the army.

5 & 6. The Rifle Brigade achieved a most striking uniform by edging their black facings with dark red. This is clearly illustrated in this painting showing a corporal and Rifleman c.1852 wearing the Albert shako and otherwise clothed and equipped like the whole Brigade on the eve of their departure for the Crimea in 1854.

7 & 8. The bugler remained a distinctive symbol of the Rifle Brigade.

9. After the Crimean War, apart from retaining their distinctive red faced, dark green uniforms, the clothes, equipment and rifle of the 60th King's Royal Rifle Corps was identical to that of the rest of the infantry, as shown here c.1858.

10. In 1873, both the Rifle Brigade and King's Royal Rifle Corps regained a distinctive item of uniform when their shakos were replaced by a short busby, as illustrated here by an officer and corporal of the latter regiment. The officers' version was made from black lamb skin, that of the rank and file of seal.

11 & 12. The busby did not last long. Both green-coated regiments reverted to the infantry's standard headgear in 1879 with the introduction of the helmet fitted with a brass spike, chain and plate, illustrated here by the Regimental Sergeant Major and a bugler of the King's Royal Rifle Corps.

the illiterate Benjamin Harris, *The Recollections of Rifleman Harris*, thanks to Henry Curling who had taken down Harris' words in 1835. Harris, an effective invalid after his combined suffering on the retreat to Corunna and then falling ill with fever on the ill-fated Walcheren Expedition, was discharged from the Army in July 1814. He subsequently earned his living at his trade of shoemaker. The final account published within living memory of the Peninsular War was that of another ranker, William Green, whose *A Brief Outline of the Travels and Adventures of William Green, Bugler, Rifle Brigade*, came out in 1857.

The final two 95th memoirs were not published until long after the deaths of their respective authors, both junior officers in the Peninsular. In 1899 the journal of George Simmons was published, *A British Rifle Man*, followed in 1901 by *The Autobiography of Sir Harry Smith*. What is remarkable of the former is that Lieutenant George Simmons maintained a personal day-to-day journal throughout the war, all of which he was able to send home during the long years of service. After the war he added further notes, effectively writing it up to make it one of the fullest of all the accounts. Further, Simmons' account meant that three soldiers from a single company, that of Captain Peter O'Hare, left their memoirs: Lieutenant Simmons, Bugler Green and Rifleman Costello--this is unparalleled amongst all the contemporary accounts. It should be added that there are various diaries and papers from the 95th that remain unpublished, for example, those of Colonel (later Lieutenant-General) William Stewart.

As to the final years of the various authors, Kincaid retired from the army 16 years after

1   2   3   4   5   6

Waterloo, being appointed in 1844 Exon of the Royal Bodyguard of the Yeomen of the Guard. In 1852 he became senior Exon and was knighted. Later he became Inspector of Factories and Prisons for Scotland, retiring due to ill health shortly before his death in April 1862 aged 75, still a bachelor. Leach remained in retirement until his death in 1855 whilst Costello survived until July 1869. As for the shoemaker Harris, his demise went unrecorded by history some time after 1835.

BERDAN'S SHARPSHOOTERS

Across the Atlantic, the American Army continued to raise formations of Riflemen during conflicts, such as the 1st through 4th US Regiments of Riflemen in the War of 1812, and the US Regiment of Voltigeurs and Foot Riflemen in 1846 for the Mexican War. Alongside volunteer units such as the 1st and 2nd Mississippi that served in Mexico, there was a penchant for units of volunteer mounted riflemen, such being utilised in the long campaigns against the Seminole Indians in Florida during the 1830s. The regular army, however, did not maintain a permanent unit of Riflemen, either on foot or mounted. Rather, like the original irregular formations of light troops first formed in the 18th century, these wartime units were officered and manned by tough characters from frontier communities who were treated with disdain by regular officers. At the conclusion of hostilities all were immediately disbanded at the direction of regular army officers drilled in the school of formal Napoleonic tactics.

By the outbreak of the American Civil War in April 1861, given that all soldiers were now armed with muzzle-loaded rifles, it seemed pointless to create a specialist unit of sharpshooters from the mass of volunteers pouring into the recruiting officers on both sides. Whilst some units, often continuing traditional titles from pre-existing militia and volunteer formations, carried the designation of sharpshooters, they were essentially armed, equipped and trained to operate as standard line infantry.

In the North, however, there was one individual who did believe there was still a role for highly skilled marksmen and he was to establish what would essentially become the last formation of specialist sharpshooters of the black powder era. Hiram Berdan had been a champion rifle shot for 15 years prior to the war and a leading figure in the sport of shooting in general. Something of a 'character', he had dabbled in all sorts of schemes prior to the war, leading many to view him as 'thoroughly unscrupulous and unreliable'. He was a gifted inventor, amongst his designs being a repeating rifle, a 'submarine gunboat' and various other gadgets. Whatever his personal veracity might have been, he was an undoubted patriot, and when the first shots were fired at Fort Sumter he immediately sought authorisation to raise a regiment of sharpshooters for the Union.

As with the original *Jäger* and rifle formations of the Prussian, Hanoverian, and British armies, Berdan intended his Sharpshooters to be an élite unit, and having obtained the necessary authorisation in June 1861 to raise the unit, the subsequent selection process was rigorous. William Ripley, an officer of the United States Sharpshooters, described how 'it was required that

7   8   9   10   11   12

a recruit should possess a good moral character, a sound physical development and in other respects come within the usual requirements of the army regulations. It was required of them that before enlistment they should justify their claim to be called "sharpshooters" by such a public exhibition of their skill as should fairly entitle them to the name and warrant a reasonable expectation of usefulness in the field. The recruit should in effect be able to place 10 bullets in succession within a 10-inch ring at a distance of 200 yards.'

Despite demanding these exacting standards, there was no shortage of qualifying volunteers. In fact, so many volunteers came forward that Berdan was authorised to form a second regiment in September 1861, Berdan being appointed Colonel of the 1st USSS, Colonel HA Post commander of the 2nd. The first regiment had 10 companies, the second eight, each company being drawn from volunteers of a particular state and thus bearing that state's name. These very specific company identities

Berdan's Sharpshooters were amongst the first soldiers to utilise true sniping rifles. Using his Prussian-style knapsack as a rest, specialist rifles such as this could hit a target up to a mile away.

also reflected the need for each to have its own particular *esprit de corps*, given that it was fully expected they would often operate as detached autonomous units.

The uniform Berdan ultimately adopted for his men was a traditional dark 'forest' green. Captain Charles Stevens of Company G, the USSS's first regimental historian, described the first issue of clothing: 'Our uniform was of fine material, consisting of dark green coat and cap with black plume, light blue trowsers, and leather leggings, presenting a striking contrast to the regular blue of the infantry. The knapsack was of hair-covered calfskin, with cooking kit attached...By our dress we were known far and wide and the appellation of "Green Coats" was soon acquired.' Whilst the cut of the kepi, frock coat and trousers generally corresponded to standard army regulations, Berdan looked to the tradition of the Prussian *Jäger* as reflected in the design of the knapsack. By May 1862 the blue trousers had been replaced by green to match the coat and kepi, and to complete the 'camouflage', black thermoplastic or 'gutta-percha' rather than brass buttons were worn. As the standard issue light blue NCO rank chevrons and trouser stripe stood out against the dark green of the clothes, light green versions, privately purchased from sutlers, were generally worn. As the war progressed, the inevitable wear and tear on the original green uniforms and difficulties of re-supply meant many Sharpshooters were wearing standard dark blue sack coats and light blue trousers by mid-1863. NCOs continued to purchase light green distinctions until the end of the war.

In terms of weapons, each volunteer brought their own, very much in keeping with the American tradition of the backwoods volunteer. Rifles, however, were no longer muzzle-loaded weapons taking a simple lead ball and it proved a nightmare in terms of logistics, given the varied calibres and types of ammunition involved. Thus Berdan requested his men be issued with the .52 calibre breechloading 1859 Sharps New Model rifle. Initially this request was ignored by the conservative-minded Ordnance Corps, who instead armed them with standard muzzle-loading Springfields, treating the two regiments as just another body of quaintly clothed and titled volunteer infantry. A subsequent display by Berdan himself of remarkable marksmanship before Abraham Lincoln gained Presidential interest and support. This ensured the rapid replacement of the Springfields with Colt revolving rifles. Whilst an advanced weapon in terms of contemporary technology, it had a nasty habit of discharging all its chambers simultaneously, and thus during May and June 1862 the Colts were replaced by the desired Sharps. As originally predicted, the Sharps proved both reliable and accurate, remaining the standard rifle of the USSS until the conclusion of hostilities.

Taking the field for the first time during McClellan's abortive Peninsula campaign of April-July 1862, Berdan's two regiments soon proved there was still a valid role for skilled sharpshooters. Whilst all regiments of infantry could now provide their own screens of skirmishers, the marksmen of the USSS were able to operate in small detached bodies. In many respects they were able to return to the original concept of the *Jäger*, operating as highly skilled marksmen armed with specialist weapons, stalking Confederate officers, NCOs and other key personnel. Their deadly fire soon earned them a chilling reputation for carrying '40 dead men' in their cartridge boxes. At Yorktown, one of Berdan's men, nicknamed 'Old Seth', established himself in a concealed position between the opposing lines. Having shot down the crew of a Confederate cannon, whilst his colleagues kept him supplied with food and water, he kept it out of action for over two days, striking anyone attempting to remove the piece. At the battle of Gettysburg in July 1863, the critical stand made by Colonel Chamberlain's 20th Maine on Little Round Top included support from a

detachment of the 1st USSS.

Like their earlier European counterparts, the USSS operated both as separate companies detached to various army corps and as a cohesive unit as required. At the battle of Chancellorsville in May 1863, as 'Stonewall' Jackson was completing his legendary flank march, both regiments of Sharpshooters, serving as a single brigade under Berdan, achieved one of the battle's few Union successes. Belatedly ordered to investigate reports of Confederate forces moving through the dense foliage of the Wilderness, Berdan's Sharpshooters operated as both scouts and skirmishers for General Birney's division as it moved south towards Catharine's Furnace. Although Jackson's main column had long since passed, the 23rd Georgia under Colonel Emory Best still held the Furnace position to cover the passage of the last few wagons. At around 1pm Berdan's riflemen began to approach the 23rd's outlying piquets and within moments bullets began to fly and Georgians began to fall.

Birney's division included a brigade of six Pennsylvanian regiments and one of its regiments stood in close support as Berdan's men pushed forward using classic tactics for specialist marksmen. They crept through the high swamp grass that bordered a shallow stream, Lewis's Run, and used various ruses to tempt the Georgians concealed amongst the trees ahead, to reveal their positions. As recorded by a Pennsylvanian observer,

This rear view of the same recreated sergeant shows the Prussian-style knapsack and tin canteen chosen by Berdan to which the sergeant has attached a waterproof poncho and an extra pair of boots.

Next page, Louis Johns' painting of the Rifle Brigade fording the Alma River in 1854 captures what was, in effect, the last time the Rifles operated as specialist skirmishers.

a rifleman would place his kepi on a ramrod to draw fire: 'He then gave a leap and fell on the grass as if dead. This caused several Rebs to look out from their hiding places...' This and other tactics succeeded in winkling out many Confederates, but it took some time for Berdan's men to begin to work their way around the Georgians' flanks and force Best to commence falling back.

As the Georgians retreated, Best left a company as a rearguard in the foundry building. The Sharpshooters ensured they bought little time, as is recorded by one of their lieutenants, George Marden: 'Whenever they showed a head they got a crack shot.' As Mardens continued, it was the Sharpshooters' chaplain, Lorenzo Barber, armed with his own Sharps, who demonstrated the range, accuracy and power of the marksmen. 'The sight of a butternut looking through a barn window at four hundred yards was too much for him...he blazed away and the rebs dropped out of sight like so many prairie dogs...In a few moments the rebs showed a white rag and came in; 56 of them including the Maj. & Chaplain.'

Although both sides were feeding fresh troops into the action around Catharine's Furnace, the Sharpshooters' relentless pursuit of the 23rd proved decisive. Best's men had gone to ground in the cut of an unfinished railroad several hundred yards to the south. The cutting served as an effective trench, but it ultimately proved a trap. Although the Georgians were able to hold the Sharpshooters away from their front, they were pinned by the accurate fire of the Sharp's and Best's men were too few to prevent Berdan's men moving around their flanks. With bullets beginning to sweep the length of the cut, Best and a handful of his men managed to escape, but most dare not expose themselves to almost certain death. Within minutes, 296 men of the 23rd, almost the entire regiment, surrendered to the Sharpshooters. From first to last, the whole action had lasted less than one hour, although it had cost the Sharpshooters almost 80 casualties.

During the Civil War, despite heavy casualties, a total of 1,008 officers and men being killed and wounded in action, sufficient volunteers continued to flow in to maintain the ranks throughout the campaigns of the Army of the Potomac. In all, 1,392 officers and men served in the first regiment, of whom 546 became casualties, whilst 1,178 served in the second, of whom 462 were killed and wounded. In the autumn of 1864, as the long siege of Petersburg dragged on, many volunteers who had originally joined in 1862 for three years were mustered out, and the two regiments were consolidated into one before finally being disbanded in February 1865, despite their sacrifice and proved utility. In keeping with the original 18th century tradition of specialist volunteer formations raised only in time of war, the USSS were disbanded at the conclusion of hostilities.

RIFLE REGIMENTS TODAY

The King's Royal Rifle Corps (KRRC) and the Rifle Brigade saw extensive service in both world wars. During the First World War, the KRRC raised a total of 26 battalions whilst the Rifle Brigade raised twenty-one battalions, suffering 12,842 and 11,575 fatalities respectively. With the coming of peace in 1919, both regiments were again reduced, first to the four pre-war battalions, then to just two battalions apiece in 1923. With the outbreak of the Second World War, there was the usual rapid expansion, the KRRC ultimately fielding 11 battalions, the Rifle Brigade nine.

As the Cold War began, the process of reduction and amalgamation set in again, both regiments being reduced to a single battalion by the mid 1950s. In 1958 'Shorncliffe' was embodied into a single regiment when the Oxfordshire and Buckinghamshire Light Infantry (the 43rd and 52nd had been amalgamated back in 1881), The King's Royal Rifle Corps and The Rifle Brigade became the three battalions of The Green Jacket Brigade. On 1 January 1966, the Brigade was re-designated

The Royal Green Jackets, a regiment of three battalions (plus two territorial battalions). Thus each of the regular battalions maintained the traditions of the three original regiments, the first battalion the 43rd and 52nd, the second battalion the King's Royal Rifle Corps and the third battalion the Rifle Brigade. There were also two territorial battalions: the fourth battalion London, the fifth battalion Oxford and Buckinghamshire.

With the end of the Cold War, *Options for Change* reduced the regiment to just two regular battalions, the first battalion being disbanded (the justification for this, it has been argued, being that the 43rd and 52nd were not originally greencoats). Although not officially recognised in any way, the present first battalion traces its lineage back to the 60th, whilst the second battalion looks back to the 95th. Finally, the 1999 reductions in the Territorial Army have seen the announcement that both territorial battalions of the Royal Green Jackets are to be disbanded.

Whilst the units that formally trace their lineage back to the British Army's first Riflemen are gradually disappearing, all modern infantrymen now reflect the ethos and training that originated with the fifth battalion 60th and the Experimental Rifle Corps, later the 95th. Today's soldier is capable of a multiplicity of tasks, trained to fight and think as an individual. They are expected to be proficient in the technology they use, have the intellectual flexibility to adapt to an ever-changing combat environment and to make use of whatever ground they find themselves engaged on – all attributes of the original Riflemen. The appeal to soldiers' self-respect and a desire to excel is the norm, a process commenced by officers like Rottenberg, Stewart and Beckwith. The role of the marksman has also survived, being encapsulated by the modern sniper. Originating in the trenches of World War One, today it is considered a specialist course, whose intensive training, specialist weapon and use of concealment echo the 18th century *Jäger* and Napoleonic Rifleman.

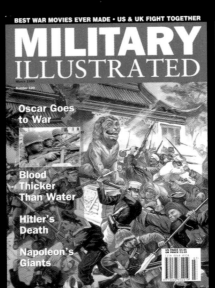 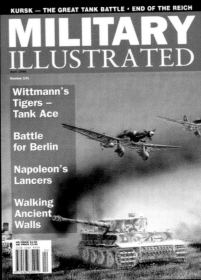
 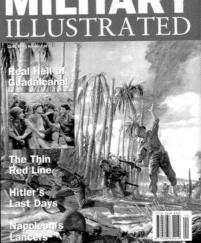

BIBLIOGRAPHY

Beaufroy, H., *Scloppetaria*, London, 1808.

Blackmore, H. L., *British Military Firearms, 1650-1850*, Greenhill Books, 1994.

Bryant, A., *Jackets of Green*, Collins, 1972.

Buchanan, J., *The Road to Guilford Courthouse*, John Wiley & Sons, 1997.

Buckley, R.N., *The British Army in the West Indies*, University Press of Florida, 1998.

Caldwell, G., & Cooper, R., *Rifle Green in the Crimea*, Bugle Horn Publications, 1994.

Caldwell, ,G., & Cooper, R., *Rifles at Waterloo*, Bugle Horn Publications, 1995.

Chambers, G.L., *Bussaco*, London, 1910.

Chartrand, R., *British Forces in the West Indies 1793-1815*, Osprey, 1996.

Chartrand, R., *British Forces in North America 1793-1815*, Osprey, 1998.

Chester, H.M., and **Burges-Short**, G., *Records and Badges of the British Army, 1900*, re-printed Greenhill Books, 1989.

Cooper, T.H., *A Practical Guide for the Light Infantry Officer*, London, 1806.

Cope, Sir W.H., *The History of the Rifle Brigade, Formerly the 95th*, London, 1877.

Costello, E., *The Adventures of a Soldier, or Memoirs of Edward Costello of the Rifle Brigade*, London, 1841.

Curling, H., *Recollections of Rifleman Harris*, Leo Cooper, 1970.

Dalton, C., *The Waterloo Roll Call*, Arms and Armour Press re-print, 1971.

Duffy, C., *The Army of Frederick the Great*, David & Charles, 1974.

Duffy, C., *The Army of Maria Theresa*, David & Charles, 1977.

Dupuy, T.N., Johnson, C., and **Bongard**, D.L., *The Encyclopaedia of Military Biography*, Tauris, 1992.

Fletcher, I., *The Waters of Oblivion: Crauford's Light Division*, Spellmount, 1991.

Fletcher, I., *The British Invasion of the Rio de la Plata, 1806-1807*, Spellmount, 1991.

Fletcher, I., *Wellington's Regiments: The Men and Their Battles 1808-1815*, Spellmount, 1994.

Fletcher, I., *Napoleonic Wars - Wellington's Army*, Brassey's, 1996.

Fuller, J.F.C., *British Light Infantry in the Eighteenth Century*, London, 1925.

Fuller, J.F.C., *Sir John Moore's System of Training*, Hutchinson, 1924.

Gates, D., *The British Light Infantry Army, c.1790-1815*, Batsford, 1987.

Glover, R., *Peninsular Preparation: The Reform of the British Army, 1795-1809*, Cambridge University Press, 1963.

Godwin-Austen, A.R., *The Staff and the Staff College*, London, 1927.

Gould, R.W., *Mercenaries of the Napoleonic Wars*, Tom Donovan Publishing, 1995.

Griffith, P., *The Art of War of Revolutionary France 1789-1802*, Greenhill, 1998.

Hall, J.A., *The Biographical Dictionary of British Officers Killed and Wounded, 1808-1814*, Greenhill Books, 1998.

Hargreaves, R., *The Bloodybacks: The British Serviceman in North America 1655-1783*, Rupert Hart-Davis, 1968.

Harris, B., *A Dorset Rifleman: The Recollections of Benjamin Harris*, Shinglepicker Publications, 1996.

Hathaway, E., *Costello: The True Story of a Peninsular War Rifleman*, Shinglepicker Publications, 1997.

Haythornthwaite, P.J., *Wellington's Military Machine*, Guild Publishing, 1989.

Hofschröer, P., *The Hanoverian Army of the Napoleonic Wars*, Osprey, 1989.

Hughes, B.P., *Firepower*, Arms and Armour Press, 1974.

Houlding, J., *Fit for Service: The Training of the British Army, 1715-1795*, Oxford University Press, 1981.

Hutton, Sir E., *Colonel Henry Bouquet 60th Royal Americans - 1756-1765: A Biographical Sketch*, Winchester, 1911.

Kincaid, Sir J., *Adventures in the Rifle Brigade, in the Peninsular, France, and the Netherlands, from 1809 to 1815*, London, 1830.

Kincaid, Sir J., *Random Shots from a Rifleman*, London, 1835.

Leach, J., *Rough Sketches of the Life of an Old Soldier*, London, 1831.

Lehman, J.M., *Remember You Are An Englishman*, London, 1977.

Lowell, E.J., *The Hessians and the other German Auxiliaries of Great Britain in the Revolutionary War*, Corner House Publishers, 1975.

Ojala, J.A., *Auguste De Colbert*, University of Utah Press, 1979.

Oman, C., *Sir John Moore*, Hodder and Stoughton, 1953.

Oman, Sir C., *A History of the Peninsular War - 7 Vols.*, Oxford, 1902-1930.

Page, F.C.G., *Following the Drum: Women in Wellington's Wars*, Andre Deutsch, 1986.

Pakenham, T., *The Year of Liberty: The Great Irish Rebellion of 1798*, Hodder & Stoughton, 1969.

Paret, P., *Yorck and the era of Prussian Reform*, Princeton University Press, 1966.

Pelet, J.J., *The French Campaign in Portugal 1810-1811*, edited, translated, and annotated by Donald D Horward, University of Minnesota Press, 1973.

Pivka, Otto von, *Brunswick Troops 1809-15*, Osprey, 1985.

Raynor, K., 'Private, 95th (Rifle) Regiment', *The Age of Napoleon*, No.23 Partizan Press, pp.14-17.

Reid, S., *King George's Army 1740-93: (1) Infantry*, Osprey, 1995.

Reid, S., *British Redcoat 1740-1793*, Osprey, 1996.

Reid, S., *British Redcoat (2) 1793-1815*, Osprey, 1997.

Rigaud, Major-General Gibbes, *Celer et Audax*, Oxford, 1879.

Ripley, W., *Vermont Riflemen in the War for the Union 1861 to 1865: A History of Company F First United States Sharp Shooters*, first published by Tuttle & Co 1883, reprinted by the Grand Army Press, 1981.

BIBLIOGRAPHY

Rothenberg, G.E., *The Art of Warfare in the Age of Napoleon*, Batsford, 1977.

Baron Francis de Rottenberg, *Regulations for the Exercise of Riflemen and Light Infantry*, 1803 edition.

Siborne, H.T., (ed), *The Waterloo Letters*, Arms and Armour Press re-print, 1983.

Simmons, G., *A British Rifleman: the Journals and Correspondence of George Simmons, Rifle Brigade, during the Peninsular and the Campaign of Waterloo*, London, 1899.

Smith, Sir H., *The Autobiography of Lieutenant-General Sir Harry Smith*, London, 1901.

Surtees, W., *Twenty-Five Years in the Rifle Brigade*, Greenhill Books, 1996.

Verner, W., *History & Campaigns of The Rifle Brigade 1800-1813*, London, 1905.

Wilkinson-Latham, C., *The Royal Green Jackets*, Osprey, 1975.

RIFLEMAN DIRECTORY

Museums

The Royal Green Jackets Museum, Peninsular Barracks, Romsey Road, Winchester, SO23 8TS, has the world's most extensive collection of original items and illustrations relating to both the 60th and 95th Rifles. In particular, almost half the museum is given over to a fine display telling the story of the 95th Rifles during the Napoleonic Wars, detailing both their innovative training and many battlefield exploits.

The National Army Museum, Royal Hospital Road, Chelsea, London, SW3 4HT, has a number of original uniform and equipment items of the Rifles as well as some fine examples of the Baker rifle itself.

The Royal Armouries Museum, Leeds, is essential to anyone interested in the evolution of the rifle itself, from its earliest manifestation in the 16th century through to the present day.

Re-Enactment Groups

For those interested in taking their study of the Rifleman beyond the armchair, there are a number of re-enactment groups specialising in their portrayal.

Old France and New England recreate the soldiers and warfare of the French-Indian War of 1755-60. Its members include early British light infantry, Colonial Rangers and even Woodland Indians. Contact: Ralph Mitchard, 54 Lower Whitelands, Radstock, Bath, BA3 3JP. Tel 01761-437543. E-mail ralph@rmitchard.freeserve.co.uk.

The Fifth Battalion, 60th Royal Americans circa 1808-15 are recreated as they would have appeared and operated in the Peninsula 1808-14. This group prides itself on being fully equipped with reproductions of the legendary Baker rifle. Contact: Dennis Wraight, Flat 11, Marlborough Court, Marlborough Hill, Harrow, Middlesex, HA1 1UF. Tel 0181-861-0830.

The 95th Rifles circa1808-15 are recreated by various groups, contacts include:

Les Handscombe,
48 Mutton Place,
Prince of Wales Road,
London, NW1 8DF.

Neil Collins,
12 Warsash Close,
Leigh Park, Havant,
Hampshire, PO9 4LE.
Tel 01705-345416.
E-mail collinsfamily@msn.com

Steve Barker,
51 Armitage Road,
Birkby, Huddersfield,
West Yorkshire, HD2 2UB.
Tel 01484-534219.

For those interested in recreating the Rifleman of the American Civil War there are two major societies in Britain. For those living north of Northampton there is the American Civil War Society, PO Box 52, Brighouse, West Yorkshire, HD6 1JQ. For those south of Northampton contact the Southern Skirmish Association, PO Box 485, Swindon, SN2 6BF

Book Suppliers

Offering the widest selection of both new and second-hand books on military history is Caliver Books, 816-818 London Road, Leigh-on-Sea, Essex, SS9 3NH. Tel/Fax 01702-73986

A long-established bookseller specialising in second-hand military books, including personal memoirs and regimental histories is Francis Edwards, 13 Great Newport Street, Charing Cross Road, London, WC2H 7JA. Tel 0171-379-7699, Fax 0171-836-5977.

Reprinting numerous works and publishing new books on Napoleonic military history is Greenhill Books, Park House, 1 Russell Gardens, London, NW11 9NN. Tel 0181-458 6314, Fax 0181-905-5245, E-mail lionelleventhal@compuserve.com, Website www.greenhillbooks.com.

Providing a wide selection of both new and second-hand military history works is Paul Meekins, 34 Townsend Rod, Tiddington, Stratford-upon-Avon, Warwickshire, CV37 7DE. Tel 01789-295086.

One of the most comprehensive catalogues of military works is published free by Ken Trotman Ltd, Unit 11, 135 Ditton Walk, Cambridge, CB5 8PY. Tel 01223-211030, Fax 01223-212317

INDEX

ACKNOWLEDGEMENTS

During the research and writing of this narrative, I have had the invaluable advice of Ian Fletcher and Richard Moore, both of whom were willing to share with me their vast vault of knowledge. As to the illustrations, my thanks again must go to Ian and Richard for allowing me to reproduce a number of pictures from their personal collections. Equally, to the ever-generous willingness of English Heritage and the Wallace Collection in permitting me access to their picture collection. I must also acknowledge the considerable assistance of the National Army Museum and Major Grey of The Royal Green Jackets Museum in enabling me to utilise pictures from their respective collections.

My thanks must further go to the generosity of the various re-enactors who were willing to give their time freely (often in adverse weather conditions), to enable me to take photographs, particularly members of the 60th Royal Americans. Finally, but far from least, I am as ever in the greatest debt to my wife Caz for her willingness to check and correct my often faulty grammar and for her patience with my long hours in the study.